WHAT I NEED FROM YOU: The essential guide to reaching troubled teens

SAM ROSS

Published by Teenage Whisperer Press

First Printing, 2019

_____

Teenage Whisperer

contact@teenagewhisperer.co.uk

www.teenagewhisperer.co.uk

_____

ISBN: 9781728812144

For Cade as you start your journey seeking to understand, connect and help others. I couldn't be prouder!

For all the young people I have worked with who have each in their own way taught me something new about how best to hear them and to help them grow.

CONTENTS

WHAT IF WE UNDERSTOOD?

They are the impossible ones, the unworkable ones. The ones that refuse to be helped. The ones that take your words of encouragement and help, stack them up and light a match and laugh as they watch them burn. You wonder if they care. You sometimes get to the point of wondering if *you* care.

What's the point? They are a lost cause.

But something niggles. Something stops you from emotionally walking away. But what can you do? You've tried everything and it's failed.

Or maybe you are about to start working with challenging teens and you desperately want to make a difference and want to avoid making mistakes. But how?

It would be great if we could just ask these young people and get an answer. If you are experienced in working with teens, 'What can I do to help?' are words that you will probably have said.

They were probably said in a positive tone at the beginning of your work with that young person, when you thought there was some hope, but that probably gave way to an utterly exasperated, desperate tone as you ploughed your way through your usual strategies, your usual intervention programs and seemingly got nowhere.

The challenge for the most troubled teens in answering the question, 'What can I do to help?', is that they often do not know the answer. For starters, they often don't know what's wrong in the first place. They know on one level that their life is all over the shop, but they have no idea how they got there and no idea how they really feel about it. Even if they do know what's wrong, they often have no idea of how to express it.

Add to this their ambivalence about whether they want to go to the effort of changing their lives and whether things could be any better even if they did try, and you have the perfect formula. The perfect formula for them to sit in silence, to grunt, or to tell you where to go and if you're very lucky, to do all three in ten minutes. It's basically all too much, and that's when only considering the question of what's wrong.

If we then ask them to consider what would help them, we are asking an even more complex question that requires a level of self-awareness and understanding that they often just do not have. They are so consumed with the task of surviving in a world that has not treated them well or has not met their needs or that they have never learned how to navigate well, that they do not have the emotional or mental bandwidth or the thinking skills to deal with such higher order questions.

So what are we to do? If they can't or won't tell us what's

wrong, or tell us how to help them fix it, what can we do? If they're not talking, or not even turning up to meet with us, we're stuffed aren't we?

Well, no. This is the point where my Teenage Whisperer blog started, over five years ago.

What if they could tell us? What if we could understand why they were behaving in such a challenging way? What if we could then understand what they needed in the here and now so that they would start to engage with us? So that we could together find out what would make life better? Make them feel better? To behave more constructively for themselves? To start to make changes and to finally start engaging with life, to start really living?

So I started to write, sometimes in my own voice, and sometimes in the voice of a troubled teen and once I started, I couldn't stop. All the teens I have worked with, all the teens I have asked to tell me of their experiences of working with professionals, and all the teen voices that have often got lost in the academic books and research I have read, coalesced into an orchestra of voices that wanted you to hear what they needed from you. Voices that wanted to say what so many real-life teens are unable to say. And judging by the response to my blog, voices that you, as people working with these teens, and also struggling parents, want to hear.

And most importantly to me, these voices, including my own, don't just tell you how it is, or how it feels, or how many people are affected- they tell you what you need to *do* in light of this, what you need to *do* to help overcome their challenges and their issues. To my mind this is where understanding as a lived experience rather than a theoretical idea really starts. Knowing what the problem is, isn't enough. Knowing what to do in light of that information is where understanding truly begins and where change becomes a possibility.

If you take just one thing away from this book, I want it to be this:

Troubled teens don't want you to merely know them, they don't want you to merely hear them- they are in desperate need of people who will take the time and care to understand them and to meet their needs.

So what follows is a collection of my writing that will hopefully help you to do just that.

I in no way wish to replace or question the value of the astoundingly brave and important growing body of writing by actual teens themselves (see www.pongoteenwriting.org to read some amazing pieces of teen writing and to find out more about the transformative effect of writing for troubled teens). I am in debt to these young people as much as those that I have worked with for increasing my understanding of what it is to be a troubled teen.

> Troubled teens are in desperate need of people who will take the time and care to understand them and meet their needs.

What I seek to bring to the table when I write in the voice of a troubled teen is further insight from an academic and professional perspective that is accessible and emotionally engaging as the writing of teens themselves. The world needs academic books, but sometimes we need the academic to be more imbued with the stuff of real life- with the rawness of humanity, of emotion and the ability of words to paint pictures as well as to state facts, report research findings and theories.

4

At the end of the day, the rawness and the emotion is what we respond to. It is what gets us out of bed in the morning to go and meet with our troubled teens. It is what makes us persevere, no matter what. It is what makes us want to know more, to do better, to do right by them. We don't push on against the odds because somebody told us to. We push on because we feel. On some level we are emotionally affected by their pain, and our natural human response is to persist in trying to help them.

So my writing is not just about informing you. It's about helping you to understand, to feel, and to respond. Because it is when our troubled teens see that we feel, that we are human, that we care, that we want to understand, that they start to become interested in us and entertain the idea of actually engaging with us. It is because we are giving them what they crave for most in this world- someone who is listening and is genuinely interested in them. It is only then that they will come and be willing to work with us.

What follows is an essential guide to what we need to do or show them to get them to that place where they know we care and are willing to let us help them change their lives for the better. Each chapter, in no particular order, covers a particular need that our troubled teens desperately need us to meet if they are ever going to get to that place, ranging from seeing your compassion and being affected by your positivity, to their need for you to provide boundaries and reality checks.

Be warned, there is some swearing. It's not there to shock, but in order to prepare you for the reality of working with these young people. They will sometimes use it to shock, or sometimes just because it is their everyday language. But please don't let it get in the way of building a relationship with them because that is what they need first and foremost.

This is such important work. If we don't do it, chances are no-one else will. In a world where people unfortunately find it easier to turn their backs or shout 'scum', where nothing changes in these young people's lives, we are desperately needed to show these young people and the rest of the world that they are not lost causes, they are not worthless, that they can be more than their pasts, they *can* change.

By showing them all the characteristics in this book we not only learn how to reach them, but we model what it is to be a force for positive change in this world. Gandhi said, "Be the change you want to see in the world". If we do this, we will not only change our corner of the world and change the lives of troubled teens, but *we* will change in the process. This is what we *all* need, and most of all our troubled teens.

So go be a force for good and for change. In my experience, it's the most rewarding thing you can do.

STAYING CONNECTED

This book started its life as a handful of blog posts on the Teenage Whisperer website, *www.teenagewhisperer.co.uk*

The website with its blog and resource pages aims to help all those who live or work with teens become teenage whisperers- people who can relate to, understand and help teenagers break out of negative behaviour cycles so that they can truly flourish. Its focus is very much on the practical business of engaging the most challenging teens. If you like what you read here then chances are you'll like what you read on the website too!

The website also has a resources page with lots of further reading on the topics outlined here and resources to use with young people:

www.teenagewhisperer.co.uk/resources

I have a fantastic troop of followers on social media and we regularly interact with each other providing support and resource ideas. I also regularly post the latest news items and research findings that are relevant to working with teenagers. Please join us.

 Teenage Whisperer

 @Teen_Whisperer

 linkedin.com/in/teenagewhisperer/

MY CONSUMPTION, YOUR COMPASSION

I'll hide. I'll hide with all my might from having to face this thing, to admit this thing. And I'll hide it from you with all I've got, under as many layers of antisocial behaviour that I can muster. In fact I'll do it so well that most people miss it. Hell, I can bury it so well that even I miss it.

So all people see is the binge drinker, the user, the offender, the antisocial scum, the lout, the gobby one, the violent one, the one who doesn't give a crap, the one who seems to be devoid of care, of feeling, lacking in common decency, common humanity.

What people find hard to see, what I don't want to see, don't want to have to acknowledge and process, is the pain that courses through my veins. The emotional pain that consumes me. Of life disappointed, of fundamental human needs unmet, of experiences that have skewed my view of the world, of others, of me. A pain that drives me, controls me, brings out the worst and not the best in me.

It's not an excuse, but it is my explanation. I know other people have seen the things I've seen, felt the things I feel and they manage not to take it out on the people and places around them. Maybe they've had people in their lives- parents, carers, teachers, youth workers- who have cared enough to teach them appropriate coping skills, have shown them how to respond to challenging experiences with dignity, in a constructive rather than destructive way. Or maybe they've only turned their pain inwards rather than outwards and expressed in the purge or the cut or in other ways. Some go inwards, some go outwards, some do both, but we have all drunk from the same well of pain.

Problem is, it is easier to see pain and to want to see it when the behaviour doesn't detrimentally affect others. The quieter the expression of pain, the less in your face it is, the less harm that is caused to others, the more compassion and understanding is on offer.

When I blow outwards, when I lash out, when I destroy, when I hurt others, I test the limits of sympathy, of compassion. But what if you could actually see the pain, acknowledged or unacknowledged that drives my actions? Would it be easier to see past my obnoxiousness for what it really is? If I went around on crutches would you hold open the door for me? Would you offer to help?

My crutches are there, but people often don't see them as that. They are the emotional crutches that get me through the moment, the hour, the day, the week. They are just as real as the ones that keep the kid with the broken leg mobile. They're just harder to see; I don't see them for what they are, and neither do most other people. Blowing my top to relieve some of the internal pressure, looking for fights to express my frustration, taking drugs or drinking to help me forget, to mask the pain, robbing people for a buzz, as a pick-me-up. I'm not being a shit just to be a shit, there is a pain that drives me to survive in whatever way I can.

Somewhere deep, deep down, often so deep down where I can't initially reach, I know that my way of coping is wrong. I know that this does not help me. I know it harms others, but I don't know what else to do. I don't know how else to get through the day, to get through my life. And if any sense of guilt or shame surfaces, I do not have the ability to process that either, so I'll drink some more, offend some more, and bury that deeper down, along with the rest of my pain.

Sometimes I'll have flashes of insight, I'll realise I'm in a bad place and that there's stuff I should do to at least try and sort it. Stuff that would help. But I just can't. That's why I'll say in one moment that I'll get the help, get a job, go see that person, and in the next will do the exact opposite, will return to my usual way of dealing with things. I'll drive you mad.

You see, I'll do whatever comes easiest, and continuing with my usual way is what is easiest to me right now. It might seem that my escapism takes more energy than doing the right thing, all the stuff that would actually help me. But it's not about physical energy, it's about mental and emotional energy, and I'm all out.

And that's why people, even those who initially wanted to help, look at me and my behaviour in disgust or despair and declare that I'm thoughtless, I clearly don't understand what I am doing, or I do and just don't care how it affects myself and others. And they'd be right. That's the whole point.

I don't want to think; thinking takes mental energy, and I don't have any of that. I just do. Do what is there, what is easy, follow my crowd, act on impulse, do whatever it takes to feel a little bit alive, a little bit better about myself, do whatever it takes to avoid having to feel and address my pain. So even if I can see something better, more constructive, I lack the emotional energy to see it through. And you get frustrated. You have moved heaven and earth to create an opportunity for me, and I throw it back in your face. Little by little, I become a lost cause, beyond help. I am unlovable, unwanted, unfixable broken goods.

But this is nothing new to me. This is the easy route for me, to have confirmation of my undesirability. At least I know how rejection works. What you already know is what's easiest right? Stick with what you know, at least life is predictable that way.

In a perverse way, even if I'm driving stolen cars at 90mph, high as a kite, I feel more safe than properly trying something new and constructive, laying myself out for more potential disappointment or pain. So I'll stick with the pain I know, or the pain I'm so used to living with I don't even really notice it, rather than potentially adding to it.

So how do you get me from going with what's easiest and most damaging, to what's harder but ultimately healing? How do you get me to acknowledge and address my pain when it's the one thing I will run the hardest from?

First, you need to **see beyond what the naked eye shows you**. I may not have blood running down my face, scars on my arms. I may not have bandages, a cast, crutches or a wheelchair, but I am in pain. I am broken. I'm harder to like, harder to love, but I need someone to care enough to go beyond the obvious. Nobody behaves badly from a place of wholeness, of happiness.

Second, you need to show me the one thing that is in the shortest supply and for most goes against the grain- **show me some real compassion**, show me that you actually deep down care. Not the short-lived, conditional sort that dissipates as I frustrate the hell out of you, but the stuff that sticks. The stuff that suckers onto me and won't let me go, whatever I do. The compassion that many think I don't deserve. The compassion that I think I don't deserve. Help me to

see glimpses of the seemingly impossible. The compassion that sees the broken me and not just my broken behaviour.

It might be a cup of tea, it might be help moving, a ride to the bus station, showing up for an appointment with another agency or unexpectedly turning up to support me in some activity. It's the **going above and beyond**. As soon as you do more than your strict job description, more than any other person, worker or carer has done before for me, you show you care. I may throw it back in your face, I might not know how to deal with such positive attention, but any shard of compassion I see from you will make it easier for me to potentially come back again, to see you as a potential source of help.

And when you **persist with your compassion even when I don't treat you right**, I will come to realise you are different. I then get to a place where I might let my barriers down enough to trust you, get to a place where I might listen to what you have to say and will let you try and help me improve my situation.

This doesn't mean you should let me get away with treating you badly. If you **enforce boundaries in an environment**

of compassion they become boundaries of care rather than boundaries of rejection. Boundaries that are explained well to me will not hurt me; they will be a rejection of my poor behaviour and not me. I will come to see them as the tools of compassion rather than weapons, used to provide the stability and consistency I so desperately crave in my chaotic world. They will not drive me away, they will draw me in closer.

Once I have established that you actually care, that you are safe, then I might begin to acknowledge that maybe everything isn't as fine as I make it out to be. It becomes easier to cut through the bravado that I wrap myself in. But I won't just suddenly emotionally strip off in front of you. No chance.

I've got through life by being hard. By being the obnoxious one; no-one can touch me then. No-one will mess with me, no-one can hurt me. And the best way in, the best way to help me shed this bravado is to meet me where I am at, to tap into my toughness, to **start talking to me about this bravado thing I am good at.** It'll get me talking which is half the battle.

So start talking about when each of us has physically hurt ourselves. When you've burnt yourself on the oven, when you broke your arm, your nose, your finger. I might tell you about the time that I got stabbed in the butt. The time I got my nose broken. The time I skinned my leg coming off my scooter. I'll show you a scar or two. That's the easy sharing, the stuff we see. And I'm all about bravado so I won't be able to help myself but show off how tough I am.

This can then lead us on to discussing how resilient the body is, how amazing its healing processes are. It's then a short step for me to take to start talking about our minds, how our minds will also try to process and deal with pain, will look to heal themselves. You can then show me the biggest difference between our bodies and our minds.

Our minds can't heal themselves in the same way as our bodies do, without any conscious input from us. Stuff happens inside us to heal our bodies without us being in control. We don't consciously relay a message, "Clot the blood! Clot the blood" to a cut on our hand. The difficulty with the mind is that we are more consciously in control of it, and what's worse we have to use the thing that is in pain, to try and fix itself. We are using something that is not making us feel great, to try and make us feel better.

It is unsurprising, then, that we often get it wrong, we often make the wrong decisions. We'll behave in ways that don't ultimately help us but make us feel better and in less pain in the short term- so we might use drugs, or offend, or lash out to try and make ourselves feel better, but it often just makes it worse. We end up going into survival mode, 'just coping' mode rather than dealing with the real issue, dealing with our emotional injuries.

And show me that this isn't just me, that everyone can make bad decisions or decisions that don't ultimately help them when under emotional stress. Like hiding in TV programmes, in computer games, in a few too many wines after work when life has got on top of you, when actually the real issues need to be addressed- like the unmanageable workload, the death of a close family member, financial worries. They don't have to be directly personal examples. I just need to see that I don't have three heads, that we all have a tendency towards escapism when life gets too much, even if the way you deal with life's difficulties aren't as extreme as mine.

It then becomes less risky for me to admit that maybe I am under emotional stress, that I am carrying around emotional scars, emotional pain. Even if I have suppressed my pain so well that I'm not really aware of it, at least I might begin to consider whether my actions are fuelled by a desire to escape, to avoid something. Everyone else does it in some way, so maybe I won't worry so much about feeling weak in admitting it.

You see, one of the biggest barriers you have to help me get over is my desire to stay tough; it is my defence mechanism. One of my biggest fears about admitting, facing and processing my emotional pain is that I will turn into an emotional wimp; I'll be weak and I'll be putting myself at risk of further pain if anyone sees my vulnerability.

One of the biggest barriers you have to help me get over is my desire to stay tough: it is my defence mechanism.

You have to get through to me that the more willing people are to deal with the source of their pain, the stronger they become, not weaker. The broken leg that is treated properly will end up less damaged and cause less long term pain if appropriate treatment is sought and we place our trust in others to help us.

In terms of helping me out with my emotional pain, a core part of that trust is believing that if I fall, you will help me up again. You will not declare me hopeless, useless, an unhealable cripple and leave me lying in the road, but will reach down and help me up again, resolute in the hope that I can be helped, I can progress, I can change, I can be healed. It might be a relatively quick process, it might take years. But without your hope for me, I will have none.

Once I have acknowledged my crutches for what they are,

then the healing can begin. As I acknowledge my pain my need to hide from myself lessens over time and I become less emotionally exhausted and more emotionally available to deal with the challenge of change, of trying something new and different. New coping strategies and new opportunities become interesting and enticing rather than something to run from.

And it all starts with your compassion. The seemingly undeserved compassion. The relentless compassion. It teaches me trust. It teaches me selflessness. It teaches me the best and not the worst of life. Of how life can be given generously to others, mindful of other people's needs and feelings.

People want me to change my antisocial ways but they often don't realise that I cannot be what I have not seen, what I have not experienced. Show me in yourself what I can look like. The showing of compassion can start anywhere, in anyone. Will you be that person for me today, tomorrow, next week? Will you hold open the door?

DETERMINATION

I PROMISE YOU...
I WILL TRY AND PISS YOU OFF

Drug dealers deal drugs, prostitutes deal sex… well I deal in pissing people off, and especially you. My broken self doesn't know why I'm doing it, but my lucid self can tell you now. I am testing you. I am applying the thumb screws and seeing if you'll scream, seeing if you'll run, seeing if you are a fully signed up member of the young people's helpers club.

You know, one of those social workers, youth workers, justice workers, teachers, mentors, counsellors, you know, one of those safe guys, the ones that actually really want to help. Cos there are a hell of a lot of half-members, the ones who actually beneath the job title and pay, really in truth don't give a monkeys about me. There are more half-members out there than you probably think- trust me, most of the people who have worked with me fall into that category. They say they'll help me, they say they care but as soon as I test them by being the most foul-mouthed obnoxious kid I can be, they run.

Thing is, their job just got a bit challenging, and a bit hard, and if they can hand me over to someone else, they will. After all they are only doing the job as a way to pay the bills not because they really want to help me. They can't be bothered with the effort of trying to find out how I tick, why I am behaving like the anti-christ on crystal meth.

The thing is, I have a nose like a drugs dog- I can smell your fake caring from the other end of the baggage carousel. And you know that if I get a whiff I will show you my worst. Cos lets face it, I don't want to waste my time going through the intervention programme motions with someone who I know will dump me before too long anyway.

So I take what little choice I have and choose to dump you before you dump me. And I do that by forcing you to tell your boss that I'm 'unworkable', that 'there is nothing left that can be done for me'. 'Thank heaven for that' is what I say. Fact of the matter is that it is *you* that is unworkable, unworkable as a successful helper for me.

If you want to help me, I have to know you are genuine and the only way I can do that is to put you in the fire to see whether you are pure gold or a poxy piece of tin. So whether you are gold or tin, expect to see some sparks fly. I build a mean fire.

The gold shows itself if you keep on coming back with your compassion and caring even when I've told you where to go so many times, even when I've treated you, others and the doors, walls and windows badly. And trust me, I'm stubborn as hell and will test you until I am completely satisfied about your genuineness. When I know you are here not for the paycheck but for the passion, the compassion, the 'don't-stop-till- you-drop' desire and drive to help little toads like me, then we might start getting somewhere.

So in short, you will need to put up with a lot of crap from me at the beginning. But know that the worse a kids behaviour is, the more damaged their story is before meeting you. So fight back and meet the greater hostility with greater compassion. We are screwed to start with, and

Know that the worse a kid's behaviour is, the more damaged their story is before meeting you. So fight back and meet the greater hostility with greater compassion.

then crappy workers mess with us some more, leading to a greater level of screwed up behaviour. By this point, we are too messed up to take control of the situation, only you can start to break the cycle by not being a crappy worker.

Once you've passed the test, you'll be surprised how quickly we mellow. We might actually start doing what we are supposed to do, much to our surprise as much as yours. And this is when you can really start to help us sort out our messed-up thinking and our messed-up behaviour.

But to get to this point of helping, you have to push your tolerance levels to the max and get through the hell that we will put you through. But this is the best thing you can do for us. This is the only way you will be able to finally help us. This is the only way that we will let you in.

Cos let's face it, who is going to open themselves up, make themselves vulnerable and pour out their guts to some worker, when they have been let down by so many people before- friends, family and workers- without first making bloody sure that this person is the real deal. And if you're not the real deal... well get out my face and go and work somewhere else.

WINDOWS OF EXPERIENCE:
HOW TO RELATE TO TROUBLED TEENS

Being able to relate to the teens that we work with has to be at the core of what we do. If we can't relate, we can't really communicate, we can't understand, we can't empathise, we can't connect, we can't build a relationship that has the potential to transform. We become therapeutic statues and our hearts become like stone. We are untouched, unchanged. They are untouched and unchanged. There is no life in the relationship.

The question is, how can we relate to teenagers whose life experiences are often so radically different from our own?

Windows of emotional experience

Think about when you do relate to someone else, when you relate to their experience. It could be anyone in your life. Were your experiences identical? I'm guessing in some cases yes, in many no. I'm sure there were similarities, but I'm sure there were probably more practical experiential differences. I'm sure that the key element of the relational experience was most likely **emotional resonance**. The circumstances may not be the same but the emotions felt were. They may have differed in intensity, but the connection, the relating, was fundamentally an emotional phenomenon.

So the person who has had to deal with the death of a loved one recently, empathises and can really relate to the pain of another person who has recently lost someone. It might not be the same relationship (e.g. the loss of a mother rather than the loss of a sibling), the closeness of the relationship might differ, but the experience of loss is what makes the connection, is what helps you to understand, to empathise.

On a less serious note, think of an advert that has really resonated with you. The one that springs to mind for me is John Lewis' 2011 Christmas advert. For those of you not in the UK, John Lewis is a department store and they have become very well known for their Christmas adverts. To watch go to www.teenagewhisperer.co.uk/WINFY.

In short, the advert tells the story of a young boy who is desperate for Christmas to come. It leads you to believe that it is because he can't wait to receive his presents. The big reveal comes when Christmas Day finally arrives and he jumps out of bed, straight past all his presents neatly wrapped, and goes into his wardrobe and lifts out a less than perfectly wrapped present and proudly walks to his parents' room with a big grin on his face. The strapline appears: 'For gifts you can't wait to give'.

I am not one to get hooked into adverts, but as a parent of young children myself this had me hook, line and sinker. And why? Because it connected with emotions I had already experienced myself- of being desperate for

Christmas to come as a child (although usually for the more typical selfish reasons), of being so unendingly proud of my children when they think of others before themselves or of the joy of receiving a slightly crooked gift that my children have made for me that is infused with love and thought… and so it goes on. Not identical experiences or circumstances, but similar emotions.

It is now seven years after I first watched this, and it still gets me. But why?

Connections based on emotion are the ones that make a lasting impression because we are fundamentally feeling beings. This applies to advertising, to any relationship we have with anybody. The ones that 'get us', that 'stick' are the ones that involve a sharing of emotion, even if it is a corporate sharing through an advert. And no less is it with our teens.

Relating to the teens in front of us is about emotional connection with them and is not dependent on us having been through their life experiences (thank God). We don't have to have experienced the same level or complexity of emotion. What we do need is a reasonable level of personal emotional awareness and an ability to use those emotional experiences to give us windows of understanding into theirs.

For example, one of my blog posts, 'My Constant Change, Your Life-Changing Constancy', about how challenging teens have probably had to endure more change in their lives than we realise such as changes of care placement or change of school, was actually sparked by my experience of moving house. Thinking about how unsettling that was for me and my family, got me to thinking about how utterly unsettling and emotionally draining all the change that a troubled teen may have to endure would be.

So while my experience was significantly different, while

the intensity and complexity of the emotions also differed, that experience gave me a little peak into their emotional lives and started a whole train of thought and exploration with teens that led to that blog post.

You can read this post at:

www.teenagewhisperer.co.uk/constant-change-life-changing-constants/

Or we might have a teen sitting in front of us and we can tell that they have a deep, deep ingrained fear of something, but we have no idea what that is. They don't want to share. Tapping into our own experience of when we might have been afraid of something in the past or present, even something as daft as being scared of spiders can help us to begin to understand their fear and therefore what might help them talk about it.

For example, if you are scared of spiders you might not want to talk about spiders even. So the best chances of getting you to talk about spiders is to make it clear that right here and now there are no spiders that are going to get you so it is safe. You then might be more inclined to talk. You then use this knowledge of your fear of spiders to help you with whatever your teens fear is. So you might say,

"I sense you're afraid of something. If so, does it scare you to even talk about it?"

To that you might get a nod, so then you definitely know there is something they are afraid of and then you can discuss ways that might help them to feel safe enough to talk about it.

Most of the time our windows of experience are something that we never actually share in our sessions. They are just there as we contemplate our teens and try to find points of connection & understanding of their experience, from what they have told us or what we might have read in their file, as a means of working out what is going on in their lives, in their heads, in their hearts, and what might help us understand them better and practically help them.

The emotional connection is still there even if it is not explicit as it will be evident to our teens through our words and actions and the care that we demonstrate. If they can sense that we are trying to 'get them' to understand them, then they know we are emotionally as well as professionally invested in them (through our care) and the relationship will grow.

Use your own emotional experiences to gain windows of understanding into theirs.

Sometimes it is appropriate to share our experience, although this has to be done with the right intention, with sensitivity and never losing sight of the fact their sessions with us are about them, not us.

So using the change example again, if a teen is about to experience another change themselves and seems really down about it but isn't very communicative, I might say something along the lines of,

"Change is tough, don't you think? I recently moved house and found that quite unsettling so I can guess that you might be finding this change coming up quite hard? Or are you okay with it?".

If what I am saying resonates with them, they will usually speak.

Nothing knocks down communication barriers more quickly than an exchange of personal experience, of personal emotion. If we give them a little window into who we are and our emotions, they are way more likely to give us a little window into theirs where possible.

It's important not to throw our personal experiences in all the time. We should only do it if it is going to help them express themselves, to help them open up. We also have to be careful that we are not sharing with the purpose of making ourselves feel better, but with the sole purpose of helping them.

It is also important not to project our experiences onto them (transference), as if their experience was just like ours. We have to allow them to tell their own story, describe their own experience and emotions for themselves. We should never presume to know their emotions and their experience just because we've had our own experience, whether big or small.

So regarding change, for example, we should never say something like,

"When I moved house I was so unsettled. You must be feeling the same way. Not knowing anyone, anywhere......".

Here we are telling them they should be feeling the same way we did. We are also giving them a list of things to worry about. Our windows of experience should be helping them talk more, express themselves more and the above certainly does not do this.

We should never say *"you must be"* and we should always have a statement or a question in there that gives them an opportunity to voice a different experience or emotion. For example, in the first example above, the question that allowed for a different view was, *"Or are you okay with it?"*. By doing this you give them permission to feel as they feel, a vital ingredient to a strong working relationship.

If these experience sharing pitfalls are avoided, some real

communication can occur. Whether we like it or not, we and our teens are human beings who have a natural need to emotionally relate and connect. If we don't give of our emotional selves in any way in our practice, whether in our thoughts or our practical discussions with teens we have a difficult question to consider. Do we have, or are we at least working towards understanding and connecting with our teens, or are we merely automatons meeting on a regular basis, untouched and unchanged?

CARING WITH CURIOSITY: GETTING TO THE HEART OF RELATIONSHIP-BASED WORKING

It is tempting to think that we've seen it all, or at least most of it and to switch ourselves into autopilot. We meet with our troubled teens, see a familiar set of circumstances, a familiar set of behaviours and think, 'Well this approach or that intervention worked with all those other teens, so let's run with that'.

There is nothing wrong with drawing on our previous experiences to inform our current thoughts and actions, in fact it makes a lot of sense. It is what we have learned works.

However it can also be extremely damaging. When we think we know what the task is before us, what the problem is that needs to be fixed before we have even started getting to know the person in front of us, we are undermining the working relationship before it has even begun. We are loading the young person in front of us with our own professional and sometimes personal experiences, creating obstacles that limit their ability to communicate effectively with us. When these young people are often struggling to communicate at all, we really can't be throwing up more barriers to effective communication.

When we think we know what's going on, we are at serious risk of not listening properly. Of making assumptions, of putting words in the mouth of our teens. Of rushing ahead and looking for a solution to a problem that we think we have perceived, that in fact isn't the problem at all, or isn't the *core* problem but is a symptom of it. We turn our expertise on and our ears off.

What is fundamentally lacking when we do this (and I defy any worker to say that they have not ever done this for reasons I will go into later), is a sense of curiosity.

CURIOSITY ABOUT THE YOUNG PERSON IN FRONT OF US

Who are they? What is their life story as told by them? What is their life story as told by others? What led them to be here today? How do they feel about it?

We are not the experts on a young person, on how they have experienced life- they are.

The list of questions should go on and on. We might have ideas as to what the answers might be, based on our intuition and experience, but we have to be ready to be wrong. In all of this, we are not the experts on the young person, on how they have experienced life, they are.

We might be experts (depending on our profession) on how to generally engage certain service groups or to deal with particular issues, but we are not the expert on the particular, individual young person we are working with- they are. We should never forget this. Forget this and we seriously damage our ability to reach them, engage them, communicate with them and to ultimately help them.

Yes, their perceptions of their life are subjective, but then so are our perceptions of their lives because we don't come into the relationship as a blank slate with no personal and professional back story. This is life, this is human interaction and the messiness and magic of our relationships, personal and professional. We are all viewing life through our own particular lens and just because one person's view on the same thing is not the same, does not make it any less valid.

And at the end of the day, the success of any intervention is entirely predicated on its suitability for the individual, for the individual as they view life, as they experience it. If we discount their view of it purely in preference for our 'expertise' we disempower them as authors of their own lives and seriously limit the likelihood of a successful outcome.

Change and growth enacted has to come from within the individual, we cannot impose it. We can foster it, we can encourage it, but the only way this happens is if we empower the young person. The best way to do this is to actually listen to them.

There is nothing more empowering than being heard, feeling that your voice matters. There is no better foundation to a successful working relationship and of positive change than the act of listening based on curiosity.

LISTENING AS THE GATEWAY TO EMPATHY

If we don't have the curiosity to want to find out more about a young person and to listen to them, we shut down. To begin to feel their pain and to begin to understand where they are coming from, to begin to understand why they might be behaving the way they are.

There is nothing more empowering than being heard, feeling that your voice matters.

There is a large difference between intellectually understanding how someone feels, and emotionally understanding how someone feels. For us to truly empathise we have to open ourselves emotionally to the young person, in precisely the same way we are asking them to do when we ask them indirectly or directly to open up to us. In all of this there is a beautiful reciprocity, an equalisation of the relationship, a powerful unspoken communication of trust, of care, that can lead to quality life-changing spoken communication.

THE RISKS OF CURIOSITY, LISTENING AND EMPATHY

However there is an inherent risk in all of this, an inherent vulnerability which can so often work against us doing any of this. It subliminally causes us to go into autopilot, into the 'I am the expert' mindset, the closed view, the closed ears, where we don't feel *with* our clients (empathise) and at best only feel *for* them (sympathise).

Working with challenging client groups can be exhausting. The 'flying by the seat of your pants' roller coaster ride of emotions that we are subjected to, where threat is always a distinct possibility, where volatility is a given, can be utterly draining.

So it is a perfectly natural response to protect ourselves emotionally as much as physically from all of this by disengaging, by pulling back, by going into autopilot. This is how we can gain some control over a situation that is so uncertain. We don't get burned if we don't stand too close to the fire.

However, in my experience, if we don't get close enough to the fire, we don't feel the warmth that comes from it. Yes challenging teens are exhausting, they can be downright obnoxious, but I find if I do not persist in trying to engage them, in listening to them, in empathising with them, I actually am more exhausted as I end up getting nowhere with them.

They can smell a mile off if I am not open, they can see my closed thinking writ large across my forehead, they can see the hands I have over my ears, and they can sense my power in the situation and the confirmation of their sense of 'nothingness'. The relationship is dead before it begins. They lose any shred of hope they may have had, and we all sit there crumpled in the corner, exhausted, thinking this is all so pointless and hopeless.

Yet if we accept the uncertainty around how things might pan out, and if we open ourselves up to the possibility of the warmth from the fire then slowly but surely at least some of the young people start to give off heat, and as time goes by the risk of the burn diminishes. We are warmed inside by the fact that we got close enough and made a meaningful connection. In an instant our work acquires new purpose and new vigour and we all come out the other side.

We might cycle from exhaustion to reinvigoration multiple times in a month and sometimes all in the same day, but I have always found that overall the reinvigoration emotionally outweighs the exhaustion if I refuse to give up hope, if I refuse to give up trying because ultimately somewhere in it all some warmth comes. Trying to keep a positive outlook, trying to hold onto hope is what has always seen me through the exhausted times.

USING OUR STRUGGLE TO HELP UNDERSTAND THEIRS

And in those times when we are tempted to autopilot our way through one of our caseload, we can use our apathy, our exhaustion, our frustration and our general negative feelings to actually help us empathise. Our pain is astoundingly powerful as a tool to connect with them.

What we are feeling is quite likely to mirror how they feel. Just as we are scared to get to close to the fire in case we are burnt, so are they. It is probable that they have been badly burned by volatile people in their lives. It is also probable that they have been badly burned when they stood too close to the fire expecting warmth and got burnt instead. It is quite probable that at least one of the people who burnt them was a professional like us.

So how we feel can help to inform our thoughts about a young person, to help inform what we might say to them, what we might ask them to find out how they are feeling, what they are thinking, what their view on the situation is.

And I personally find this process incredibly motivating. Negativity is transformed into positivity. From shrivelled raisins we can rise as juicy grapes!

This is what first-rate supervision should be doing for you. It should be a forum for you to talk honestly about how you feel, and to help you out the other side. It should be a place of transformative possibility for you, without fear of judgement. It will make you a better, more empowered, motivated worker.

And once again, do you notice the parallels here? What your young people need in their sessions, is what you need for yourself in your supervision sessions- a safe non-judgemental place to talk, where listening is everything and where positivity can be found. Once again, an opportunity to use how we feel, and what we want and need, to understand what our clients want and need too.

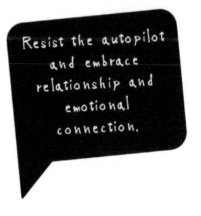

Resist the autopilot and embrace relationship and emotional connection.

And please don't go beating yourself up if you still feel like you are stuck down a big black hole and there is no way out and no amount of first class supervision or positive thinking is going to get you where you need to be. Sometimes the sheer weight of caseloads, both quantity and content, work against you being the open, engaged worker you want to be, no matter how hard you try. This is called burnout. In which case you need recuperation and restoration. You can't be giving out what you don't have for yourself (parallels again). Talk to your manager, talk to your doctor, but please don't continue to suffer in silence. You're not helping yourself and can't be effectively helping others either.

And so I suppose I end on a challenge. I challenge management, I challenge those who deliver supervision, I challenge those at the highest governmental levels. What are you going to do to ensure that those who work with some of the most challenging people can be their best? Can be available? Can avoid operating on emotionally avoidant auto-pilot? Can be curious, can listen with empathy, can empower their service users?

Tick boxes tell you nothing. Meaningful relationships can tell you everything, throughout the entire system. What are you doing to foster positive, constructive, open relationships everywhere?

And as with everything, while we might need change from the top, we can also instigate it from the bottom up. Our troubled hurting teens do not need a bunch of robot workers. What they need more than anything is someone who cares enough to be curious about them, to listen to them, to show them they are worth really knowing and to show them what a positive constructive relationship looks like. It is only by doing this that we will ever come to know what their issues are and what the right solution is for them. So we have to resist the auto-pilot and embrace relationship and emotional connection. They need it, and we need it too.

POSITIVITY

SHOW ME I'M NOT COMPLETELY CRAP

I don't deserve good things. I'm a piece of crap- I do crappy things to other people, I think crappy things. I don't deserve anything more than crap.

Crap attracts crap. I behave badly, so you'll respond in a way that confirms my feelings of crapiness. It's not a circle of life, it's a circle of crap. And there I stand in the middle, a monument to C-R-A-P, with 'loser' graffitied on the side.

From this place I find it so hard to do anything that doesn't confirm this view of myself and mostly everyone else's view of me. At least this way there are no surprises for them or me. There's a weird stability and security in choosing to swim through a river of crap rather than stand up, put some shoes on and find a nice dry sensible path to walk on. At least I know intimately what crap looks, feels and smells like. I've forgotten what a path is like, why it is worth choosing to walk there rather than swim down here.

And so I have to ask you. Please show me, please remind me where I can walk, because deep down I kind of sense that the path is the way to go. I just have no idea how to get myself from down here to up there.

And what will get me walking, or even considering the path? As pathetic as it sounds, anything that makes me feel better about myself, that lifts this weight of hopelessness, of uselessness off my chest. I can't climb out the river of crap when I'm weighed down. It's more than I can possibly manage.

But how do you begin to show me that there is something other than crap within me, that I'm not a lost cause? Simply, see the good stuff, and help me to see it too. Take off your crap-tinted spectacles that cause you to only see the bad stuff and cause me to only see it too.

Acknowledge me when I get things right. Like when I turn up, or turn up on time, or actually do some work, or do something helpful, or remember to bring something I was asked to bring. But don't do it in a skin-crawling creepish way. Or in a way that draws attention directly to me in front of my mates. I'll take it the wrong way. I may well deflect the attention by being gobby back. And you'll end up wondering why you even bother. That I really am the crap I think I am.

You can show me that you see my goodness just by giving me some positive attention when I have got it right. So if I turn up on time rather than saying in front of my mates, *'well done on getting here on time'*, (death inducingly embarrassing), just say something like *'great to see you'* or go to the door, look out and make a joke of it by saying *'where are the blood-thirsty lions?'*

This way you tell me you've noticed I've got it right but without making me squirm. And you know what? If you use humour like this every time I turn up on time or get something right then we might end up with a running joke, and me racing to get there on time so that I can come up with my own line. This is the stuff of relationship-building. And my sense of self begins to lighten. The possibility of fun and goodness, of something other than weighty crap becomes apparent.

And it's giving me acknowledgement for the little things that really makes all the difference. When you notice the little things that I get right, which let's face it, is often all I stand a chance of getting right at first, you are in some ways letting me know that you realise that I find the little stuff harder than most other kids.

I know some workers and teachers think that they shouldn't praise for things that should just be expected, that it's somehow mollycoddling me. But it really isn't. It's acknowledging that we all come from different places and it's about meeting basic human needs. We all need acknowledgment for our achievements.

For the ones who get regular positive attention and acknowledgment at home, they don't need acknowledgment for the little things in the same way as I do. Their need for positive affirmation has already been met. Instead you praise them for the bigger things. But for me and all the other kids who are  starved of positive attention and affirmation, who are portrayed and repeatedly told explicitly or implicitly that we are useless shits, that basic human need has not been met.

We have as much of a right for it to be met as any other kid and if we can't get it from our parents or carers then surely it isn't going to cost a worker or a teacher much to at least try to do it instead. Admittedly, we won't frequently get it for a 'big' thing, like producing an excellent piece of work, but if you can make us feel just an ounce better about ourselves by acknowledging when we do get the little things right, then you will probably find that we will start to step out the river of crap and will give you bigger reasons to positively acknowledge us.

Positive affirmation is addictive, everyone needs it and once we get a real taste we will search for more. So turning up on time, for example, won't be a big deal anymore, it'll become the norm. It'll go by unnoticed cause you'll be praising us for actually doing something more in our time together. Little steps out of the river will turn into bigger steps and hopefully we'll end up on the path. From little things, big things grow.

And another thing. If you despair that I can't even get the little things right, please stop and consider whether there are practical reasons why I might not be able to. **Are there things that you can practically help me with?**

Like am I hungry? Is a low-blood sugar making it difficult for me to keep control of myself? Do I have a watch? Can I tell the time? Do I have way more responsibility for parents/siblings at home than you could possibly imagine, so turning up anywhere on time, with right equipment, enough sleep and therefore enough self-control is a virtual impossibility? Am I actually, behind the scenes showing a massive heart of goodness and selflessness that goes beyond what any kid should do and I just don't have any goodness left for anyone else? Am I running beyond empty?

Do us a favour. At least try to scrape beneath the surface.

You may well find I am trying harder than you think and I am just lacking the skills and support to find out how to do my life a different, better way. Please show me some compassion. I have little for myself.

By starting out with acknowledgment for the little things I get right, you gradually **introduce me to the idea of more explicit praise**, to the direct 'well done'. It's easier for me to handle direct praise when away from my mates, but even so, at first I might not be able to cope.

Kids like me who have been starved of positivity in their lives often find it hard to handle direct explicit praise. It's like offering a half-starved child a lavish three course meal- they won't want to eat it all and besides, eating it all would make them ill. Crumb by crumb is what's needed and you just need to gradually increase the size of my acknowledgment/praise meal every time.

To speed up this process, **provide me with opportunities to get it right**. Opportunities to help, opportunities to contribute. And if you get me involved in something I enjoy and am good at, be it sport, arty activities, music, whatever, then I will begin to feel better about myself, whether I get praised or not. Chances are though that I will receive positive feedback, which will also improve my praise tolerance levels.

Don't get me wrong, I don't need an over-inflated big head. I just need my under-inflated one to get to normal size so I can function normally. You just need to introduce me to the whole idea of positivity- in how I see myself, in how others see me. Help me to see that I don't have to swim in a river of crap, that there is a better alternative, that I can make the change. I can climb out the river, stand up and walk a 'normal' path. That from my feelings of crapness, good things can come. From crap, plants and flowers grow. You just need to water me with a more positive view of myself and my potential.

PLEASE GIVE US OUR TIME

You want our lives to run like clockwork. A tight schedule dictated by funding, limits of patience, supply and demand imbalances. The timing cogs appear as a specified number of sessions or as deadlines. The 'we'll be working together for the next ten weeks' and the 'you have to sort yourself out by the end of the month or we'll have to look at moving you on'. New school, new foster care placement, new treatment, or back to somewhere old or dumped nowhere if we don't have a new attitude, a new behaviour. We have to be fixed or at least less broken by the time the clock strikes midnight.

The tick-tock is always there, the soundtrack to our time with you. Which is strange because for so much of our lives time stood still, the minute and second hands did not move. When we were being hit with hands or words, when we were being molested, time did not march on by. When someone we dearly loved died, our time stopped with theirs as we drowned in the pain and confusion. When we watched a parent cover the clock and hide in drugs and alcohol from the pain of the now and hurt of the past, we got stuck too, time and life did not proceed for us. When we sat and waited to feel loved, to be noticed, time was not an issue; we would wait for eternity.

So we do not understand your timescales, your hurry, your deadlines. Time has never hurried for us. It never went quickly when we cried out for it to. People didn't move quickly enough to see us, to protect us, to care for us. And now you are trying to fix us, hurrying is all important. But why force us to hurry when others did not hurry for us before?

Our experiences do not fit into a box of a period of time. Try and the experiences leak out. Our experiences don't just exist for us then, they also consume time for us now, each day, each hour, each breathing moment. They have moulded us, our thinking and our

This has to be our time, not your time. We need to have space to breathe, to take the time we need.

behaviour as we to try to cope, as we try to live with the leakage, to somehow carry on.

So to give us a timetable, a deadline to process and move on from our experiences, our pain, before we even start makes no sense. It would be like Prime Minister Neville Chamberlain at the beginning of the Second World War, announcing when it would end at the same time as announcing that it had started. Just like he didn't know when the war would end, you don't know when our battle will end for us and we don't know when time will be our own again either.

Deadlines concentrate the mind you say; they give us something to aim for. Problem is, deadlines equal pressure. Trust us when we say to you that for a lot of us there is enough pressure in our heads already. It might not seem like it by the way we behave, but we often do want to change, to do life differently. But we have no clue how to, and we don't know if we can, we are running scared and running on emotional empty. There is untold internal pressure already without the addition of an external clock tick-tocking in our ears. For so many of us the addition of a deadline only causes us to admit defeat before we've even started. We know we're not likely to meet the deadline so we don't even try. Why waste time on a pointless exercise? Time has already robbed us of enough.

This has to be our time, not your time. We need to have space to breathe, to take the time we need. Trying to cram as many of us onto your caseloads by limiting the time each of us has with you only limits the chances of you reaching any of us. Limiting the amount of time we have to check you out, to trust you, to decide that maybe you are someone worth taking the time and effort to work through our stuff with. You only end up limiting the possibility of healing connection. Breaking the relationship before it gets started, moving us on, only robs us of more time. It robs us of the chance, the time to reconnect with ourselves, time to process the past so we have the time and energy to build a new future.

We get that you have limited resources and inevitable time limitations but where possible we would ask you to smash the clock. Where you cannot, we would ask that you help us to see the bigger time picture.

Do not start a time limited period of intervention and make out like we will be 'fixed' at the end of it. Yes by all means encourage us with the hope of progress that will be made by the end but also help us to see that this will be an ongoing process. You are helping us start out. That way we can work with manageable bite-sized goals that are achievable.

And because you are helping us start, please at least try and ensure that there is some decent support to follow on at the end. It might mean connecting us up with a voluntary organisation or a mentor for example. But do not start something that you have no intention of helping us in some way finish. Do this and you will only end up adding to our bad experience box, that will only leak more and eat into our lives.

Where possible give us as much grace time as possible- the time to react to and process the feelings associated with trying to unravel, understand and move on from our histories. Our behaviour will often get worse for a while before it gets better. You try jumping into a well of pain and not thrashing around to save yourself from drowning. We will try and push you away, with harmful words and actions but you need to give us the grace to see it through. We need to see

that you care enough to see us through, to give us the time to grieve for that we have not yet properly grieved for, for our childhoods, our golden time that turned to lead.

So instead of declaring us a hopeless cause near the beginning due to our behavioural regression, see the hope that can be seen of us processing the unimaginable, of going through the dark time tunnel to get out the other side. Please, please give us this grace time. We have to go through it, to get through it. There is no shortcut; it takes as long as it takes.

We are no time travellers; oh how we wish we were. We cannot jump in a time machine and hit the fast forward button to get where we need to be, in the time frame you have given us.

We are the hurting teenagers of today, the stolen children of yesterday and the ones who should have hope for tomorrow. You need to give us the time to be all those things, to come to some acceptance about them, to face the time forwards more hopefully than the time behind us. But this you cannot hurry. If time heals then you need to let time pass on its own terms in our lives, not on your terms. It didn't hurry back then, it won't now either however hard you try and make it.

SHINING LIGHT IN MY DARKNESS

There is little light in my life. Nothing much makes me truly smile or makes me feel happy. In fact, nothing much makes me feel anything at all most of the time. 'Sunshine' and 'light' are not words I use to describe my life. 'Bloody hard', 'flippin' impossible', 'depressing' and 'dark' are more like it. There is little relief, no time off, even when I'm shooting up, or trying to escape and forget with shoplifting or joy-riding or etching my pain on my arms to try and feel that little bit better.

It's like there is a big dark cloud over my head, following me around, threatening to drop its load at any time and blocking any light that there might be in my life. It's bleak. It can be so, so bleak.

It can't surprise you, then, if I tell you that I often find talking to people really hard, particularly people like you who often have absolutely no idea what my life is like. It doesn't even have to be a serious conversation. I'm even talking about the small stuff, the social stuff, the '*how are you?*'s . It takes effort I don't have. It takes a desire to want to know you that I don't have. It takes more than I have to give.

But deep down I know I can't go on this way. Problem is, I have no clue how to get this dark cloud to shift. It consumes me, it devours me. It isn't just there blocking the light, it's eating it… it's like it's eating me.

So understand me when I ask you to try and break through the cloud, to reach me, curled up in the darkness. If you are to get to the heart of me then you have to cause my dark cloud to part and for shards of light to shine on me, even if just for a moment. For I need to feel some warmth. For I need to feel, period.

And please don't be fooled by me appearing to be the life and soul of the party, by me appearing to have such a great time with my friends, whether fuelled by alcohol and drugs or not. My depression can blow out as well as in. It can manifest itself in criminal behaviour, in aggressive behaviour too. I don't have to be quiet and withdrawn for that cloud to be over my head. People respond in different ways and in different ways at different times. Please always look for that cloud and look beyond the obvious.

While I may well need some medication to really help me out the darkness, you have to reach me in the first place to persuade me that I don't have to continue feeling like this and that I have options, including medication. But you have to connect with me first. But how on earth do you do this, when I am so closed, hiding from life, hiding from myself?

I won't appreciate you trying to reach me at first, that's for sure, I'll want you to leave me alone in my protective cocoon. I may well show up to sessions but there will be no emotional engagement. I might say words to make you go away, I might pretend to be angry and obnoxious to get you to flee, but make no mistake, I'm not truly emotionally engaged. I'm merely emotionally reacting to the here and now of your intrusion into my world. Once you go (if you go) the reaction will be over and I'll still be the same emotionally disengaged person I ever was.

Emotions can so often be faked so I get what I want. Emotions, and particularly the faked ones, are the ultimate tools of manipulation.

You need to help me truly reconnect with myself, to begin to feel something. And you know the easiest emotion to get me to reconnect with? It's surprising, because you'd think it would be my depression as that is what consumes me. The problem is, it distorts everything so wildly and causes the emotional disconnect, not the re-connect. The emotional reconnection tool is laughter.

Why? Because real honest laughter is something I can't fake, is something I feel physically and feel emotionally. When we laugh, endorphins, our bodies' natural painkillers, are released into our blood stream. When we laugh, cortisol, the stress hormone, decreases rapidly. So if I laugh and I get an endorphin boost and a cortisol crash, I get that moment's relief, the clouds part and the light hits me. For a split second at least, life feels good.

Laughter is the turning of the emotional key that starts the engine of change.

It then follows that I want more of this. As it is you giving me this, I will come looking for more. So I'll turn up to see you, I might even start to initiate the laughter, the joking, and before you know it I'm beginning to remember what it is to emotionally engage with my life. The fact that this first re-engagement is a positive experience means I'll start to engage with you. It means I won't be so scared if we move on to try and explore my other emotions further down the line. But make no mistake, until I emotionally re-engage, nothing else will happen on my road to getting help or changing my behaviour. Laughter is the turning of the emotional key that starts the engine of change.

So how do you bring the laughter into our work together? How do you turn that key?

In a word, humour, smattered liberally through our interactions.

It's the walking into every room with a smile on your face. It's being please to see me and telling me. It's the hope and positivity that pours out of you. When someone is like this, there is always the possibility of laughter, of play, of fun.

Humour can be found when you **express yourself in a slightly over-the-top melodramatic way**, like when I've made a major behavioural boob and you grab your head and exclaim, "Oh my days John, what were you thinking?". More smirks will come your way than you'd ever believe. I'm then emotionally engaged and you can then get down to the more serious business of actually finding out what happened, lessons that can be learned and so on.

It's also found when you **make fun of yourself or tell stories that are funny**. Calling yourself a 'wally' or a 'nincompoop' if you've forgotten something. Not being afraid to laugh at yourself not only makes me laugh but teaches me that you're human and can get some stuff wrong too. You hold your hands up and admit it, and give me a little laugh at the same time too.

I can't tell you exactly how to get the laughter into your work with me. **Authenticity is so important**. I can spot anything fake a mile off, and that includes pretend happy and jokey. Everybody is funny in different ways. And if you aren't about to win a comedy award for your humour, go looking for material to laugh about with me. Laugh over a program that you know I watch or the latest funny viral video on YouTube.

Ask me to show you or tell you something that's made me laugh recently. And if I don't come up with something, try and find out what does make me laugh and show me something you like.

The beginning of me escaping from my black cloud depends on me finding ways to laugh, to find moments of joy, not just with you, but in my life in general. This doesn't minimise the seriousness of what may be going on in my life, but it provides me with one tool for coping with it, to lift me out of it, to give me light and hope.

So show me what a happy person looks like. Show me how to have fun and to laugh even in the midst of sorting out the dark corners of my life. You then become an integral part of the relief I need, combined with the emotional engagement I need to start truly escaping my dark cloud. And it all starts with the warmth of a smile and a laugh.

PRACTICALITY

DON'T JUST TALK... DO

All you workers and therapists do is talk, talk, talk. And then you decide to mix it up a bit, and talk to me sat in a different chair. I'm bored, so very bored. 'Nah, nah, nah' is all I hear come from your mouth. I'm primed to stop listening before you even start.

Nothing ever changes when I talk, or let's be honest, when you do all the talking. I've been sat here, in this exact same scenario so many times, and nothing changes so I've given up listening. I might make some noises to make you think I'm listening, say the buzz words you want to hear, but I'm not open for business. The shutters might be up but the door's still locked.

You spend a lot of time telling me how I need to change the way I think, how I respond, how I feel. How what I'm doing isn't helping me. And deep, deep down I would probably agree with you. But that deep, deep down is so darn deep that I can't access there right now. That needs scuba-diving equipment and I don't have any and no real hope of getting any, any time soon.

But what I do have is the here and now, my hands and feet, my body. And what I don't realise, and what you often don't realise is that by doing and not just talking, I can often change what I am thinking without ever having to strap on the scuba-diving deep thinking equipment. That actions can speak so much louder than words and can teach me so much more than you just endlessly talking at me.

Like you constantly trying to boost my self-esteem by talking about how I feel about myself. Really? Do you not understand how totally counter-productive this can be? I feel crap about myself because I've internalised all the negative stuff that people have said to me or that I have created in my own mind and I believe it, and then I start to become paranoid about how others view me. Which paradoxically causes me to start being truly obnoxious as I create this persona of a hard man, a tough girl, who doesn't care about what anyone thinks when deep down I am *obsessed* with what people think of me and I feel vulnerable and insecure. I become obsessed with me and image management to ensure no one ever sees the real me.

And then you start talking to me. Start trying to find out about how I feel about myself in your vain efforts to help me feel better about myself. You start trying to change my thinking about myself, how I interpret what people say to me, how I respond, how I react, how I think. You try and CBT the crap out of me. But I am not going to let you see the real me. So I'll turn off, I'm not interested.

The only way to get through to me and actually boost my self-esteem is to help me to stop obsessing about myself. And the best way to do this? Get me looking outward rather than inward, and this is going to require actions, not just words.

Get me involved in activities where I have a chance to help others. Something as simple as being allowed to help my teacher get books out the cupboard to something bigger like getting involved in a community project to clear up a litter-strewn area, or raising money in a charity car wash. Rather than me existing on the badly-behaved edges of society, get me involved. And you will see my self-esteem rise as I receive positive feedback for the good things I do. And over time you will see a transformation as my thinking gradually changes from being obsessed about me, to thinking about others and how to help them. The outward looking 'helping' buzz will infect me, colonise me until the bad thoughts get drowned out by good ones. Get me to this place of looking out so that I can get some perspective and see that there is more to my life than what is going on in my head.

Or if I have high levels of stress and anxiety which is why I keep on blowing up in everyone's faces, show me how to de-stress. Show me how planting lettuce or flower seeds and nurturing them to full growth can chill me out, how going to the gym can help me sweat my stresses out, how conquering a rock face can help me realise I can conquer myself. You don't teach me these things by *just* talking about them. You teach me by getting me doing.

So often, once you have got me feeling differently, I will start to think differently and sometimes it will be useful at this point to explicitly look at my thought patterns. Then I can understand a) what I was originally doing and why, and b) why this new way of thinking is helping me, and c) how I can avoid falling into those traps again, and d) how I can apply this approach to other areas of my life. If the doing comes first, talking about the thinking then becomes more relevant and interesting to me.

And you know what? Sometimes you won't even really need to do much of the talking bit. Sometimes the doing is enough to get me back on the right path, to reset my thinking and my outlook.

If you do need to talk, please remember that talking about my thought patterns, even after some action enlightenment, is still not necessarily that interesting to me. Nine times out of ten my mind will wander because sitting still and listening to you is not my natural learning style. Whether I have ADHD and the characteristic ants in my pants or not, it is likely that I will engage better if we do something as we talk.

If you are involved in one of my practical activities like going to the gym, the opportunity to talk will often present itself right there and then. I'll be feeling good about myself and will be most open to hearing what you have to say.

If you're not with me during one of my activities and have separate talking sessions with me, crack open a pack of cards, play Jenga, play table tennis or pool if you have the facilities, make something, model clay, do some colouring, but please do something with me. Even people who like to talk often do something at the same time.

When was the last time you had a chat in boring room with nothing to distract you at least slightly, so that you could look down or momentarily focus on something other than the topic of conversation? That's why you go for coffee or go for a walk with your friends. This is exactly what I need too. It reduces the pressure, the tension and increases my ability to talk and focus on what you want me to talk about. Remember, doing while talking equals more sharing, which is so important if you are to really get to know how I tick and how you can help me.

Words and talking don't have even half as much effect as action. Be the practical one. It is most likely to be my language and I will remember what you have shown me and what you have helped me to discover for far longer than what you have told me. That way you equip me for always, and not just for now.

Doing while talking equals more sharing.

Don't get me wrong, words are important, but me and words have some old beef. They have been used as weapons against me, they have been used as instruments of boredom torture. In short, they haven't helped.

Actions on the other hand are more my thing. They speak to me in a way that words often can't. They help me access my thoughts in ways that words often can't. They help me learn new things in ways that words often can't. And they will help you to help me in ways that words often can't.

DO YOU CARE ENOUGH TO STOP ME?

I'm like a toddler. I have tantrums like a toddler; I swing from ecstatically excited to belligerently uncooperative depending on how the mood takes me. The crux of it is that just like a toddler I haven't learned self-control. Yes I might be more complex than a toddler in many ways, but hold onto this base fact, it can offer many clues on how you should deal with me.

Just when solving a seemingly intractable problem, a scientist returns to base principles and works on from there, so too should anyone working with a teen like me. And what is the first thing that any toddler 'manual' will tell you in dealing with an erratic tot? **Boundaries, strong and true, consistent and unshakeable**.

Yes I will probably hurl myself at a lot of your boundaries like a battering ram at the castle gates or I will nonchalantly try to breach them by pretending to be an uncaring passerby who then quietly tries to dig a hole under the surrounding walls. I do not like boundaries, and particularly the ones that I think are stupid, which pretty much means all of them. I've got on just fine ignoring boundaries so far, so why should I start paying attention to them now?

Well I'll tell you why. **I need boundaries to know that you care**. If there aren't any consistent boundaries, I know you don't give a crap. People in my life have never really enforced any boundaries consistently, so I knew that they didn't care. I just did what the hell I wanted. It was a buzz, but it didn't give me what I really needed or wanted- a sense of security, a sense of knowing what to expect, a sense of consistent care. Sometimes they'd be all police-enforcer and they'd go mental, next time they wouldn't really take any notice.

So all in all the impression that I got was that they were unpredictable and that they only cared about my behaviour when it was bothering them, not because my behaviour needed to be changed for my benefit. Basically, as I said, they didn't really care for me.

The strength and consistency of your boundaries shows me the strength and consistency of your care for me.

So the strength and consistency of your boundaries shows me the strength and consistency of your care for me. If you spell out clear boundaries and expectations to me and enforce them consistently, I will eventually warm to you because I will feel secure.

This won't be an easy path, let me warn you. I will fight

against any boundaries- that's what I've always done and while it usually gets me my own way in the short term it doesn't give me what I really need. It will take me a while to work this out and I will throw myself at the boundaries you set, I will try and break them down. Or I will try and undermine them by subtly digging under them. But by you standing strong and not giving in I will come to realise that you care- the conclusion I never got to with anyone else who put up half-baked crappy boundaries that fell with the slightest push.

So instead of boundary enforcement being a stick matter, it becomes a carrot one. As soon as I feel positive emotions that I desperately need and desire then hell, I will start to pay attention! I will have security and a sense of control because I will know what to expect if I mess up. I will at least subconsciously feel that in some way you care, and oh how I crave that.

If you have set a boundary it is also really, really important that I know what the consequence will be if I don't adhere to it. **Actions have consequences**- another lesson for toddlers that I need to learn too. That way not only I will know what is coming if I mess up, but you will be able to stay calmer and more in control of the situation because you aren't having to formulate a consequence in the heat of the moment. It also means that it is way more likely that the consequence will be fair and proportionate and not overly punitive because you are mad with me in the moment.

Being overly dramatic in your enforcing will just turn me right off. I'm used to people doing that and it will only make me angry and make things twenty times worse. Just cool and calmly explain to me when I've overstepped the line, why you have to enforce the boundary, remind me of the consequence and make it clear that this is how it will be. Make it clear that you hope it won't happen again. This shows me you see a future in our relationship and that my one screw up doesn't mean it is all ruined. After all, just like a toddler it will probably take a little while for me to learn.

I really can't argue with you when you've been mega-clear and mega-calm. Even if I do erupt at the time, I will calm down and will eventually accept that you are being fair and just, and heck, I need some of that. I will come to respect your boundaries and you.

Whatever you do, don't be overly punitive in how you deal with me. If the consequence does not match up to the action then I will just view the whole thing as unfair and will stick my fingers up at it, no matter what the consequences might be. You see, you can't socially ostracise someone into behaving when they are already socially ostracised. It's like threatening to chop a snake's hands off for stealing. It just makes no sense.

Fair enough, you might work in a system, like the youth justice system that has legal boundaries and court imposed consequences. You must impose the boundaries of the supervision sessions even if you think that the consequence of breaching me from my court order may be over-the-top. You can use your influence though, and if you think that there is a fair and just method of dealing with me then scoot yourself down to court and tell them so, or put it in your court report. At least I will then know that what you wanted for me was fair, even if what the court imposes is not. This way by enforcing the boundary you'll teach me how in society that you have to respect the law and abide by the decisions of the courts whether you agree with them or not, and at the same time show me that even though I've stuffed up, that our working relationship hasn't been flushed down the pan. The fact that you have tried to use your influence in helping the courts come to a fair decision about the consequences of my actions, shows that you care.

This is all I want in the world. To know that someone actually cares what happens to me. And the best way I know to test how much you care, is to test your boundaries. If you didn't care, you wouldn't bother to enforce the boundaries consistently. If you didn't care then you wouldn't go to the effort of thinking of suitable consequences for breaching those boundaries.

Once I know you care, then I will begin to tow the line with your boundaries. I will learn the self-control needed for me to get positive attention for living within the boundaries rather than getting the negative attention for living outside the boundaries. This is one of the biggest life lessons you can teach me and will really help me get on with the world and its systems and restrictions rather than constantly trying to blow them up with my volatile behaviour. I'm really quite simple and straightforward in many ways. If I can see the benefit of doing something, then I will.

So just like a toddler you can mould my behaviour with the food I really want and need- in my case the carrot of care. Try feeding me some, I promise I will ask for more.

DON'T TALK ABOUT ME... I'M NORMAL

You want me to change, right? Well just like you don't try to get a baby to run before he can walk, you don't try to get me to change until you've done the basics with me. And the absolute basic I have to 'get' before change is even a vague possibility, is that my life as I am currently living it is not 'normal'. Most of what I have seen and experienced in my life should never be considered anywhere near that.

And in trying to help me see this, you really have your work cut out cos I am the King of Normalisation-town. Show me the most screwed up, messed up thing, and I will make it normal. It's survival. Mental survival in its basest, purest form.

Normalising the crap in my life keeps me sane. Never mind whether it is in fact normal, hell it keeps *me* normal. No-one wants to feel like a freak. I just want to fit in, to be like everyone else. If thinking everyone else experiences the stuff I do makes me normal, then that is what I will do.

So if you try and tell me that something in my life is not normal, expect some flak; some serious fireworks in your face. Cos when you tell me that my life is not normal, you are telling me that I am not normal, and no way do I want to sign myself up to that freak club. Like it or not, the crap in my life is part of my identity. If you start messing with my perception of my life, then you are messing with my identity, which is just about the riskiest thing you can ask anyone on this planet to do, let alone a comprehensively messed up person like me. Think a minute, how would you like it?

Don't get me wrong, that doesn't mean that you shouldn't try to get me to see that my life is not normal. Cos as I said before, you won't be able to get me to change my behaviour until I do. My behaviour, my 'acting out' as you professionals like to call it, is a response to what I have experienced.

You see, even though I have normalised stuff in my life to make it more bearable, I still do, deep-down really know that what I have experienced is NOT normal. So I've got this whole inner conflict thing going on, or inner turmoil- 'cognitive dissonance'. My attempts at normalisation and the subsequent inner conflict this causes are like a boiling pan that keeps on spilling over, making a hell of a mess. And the daft thing is that I will keep on trying to shove the mess, my behavioural eruptions, back in the pan and label them normal too. My desire for inner logical consistency forces me to do this. I have to normalise everything for my alternate reality to work. Problem is that this is no long term strategy. The pot will end up boiling over big time, and my 'normal' world will fall apart.

At this point you are probably thinking that you should just give up- far too complicated, too messed up. You need to address this issue, but if you do I will see it as a personal assault and will erupt in your face. If you don't address this issue, then my behaviour will not change and you won't really achieve much with me and I'll probably erupt anyway. I guess that's why I get called 'unworkable' so much.

But there is a way. It's cunning, but it's one of the best ways to get me to see my life for what it is. **Don't talk about me**.

Tell someone that their life is not 'normal' and you get their backs up immediately. It is a moral judgement and it is patronising as hell. And what teen do you know that likes to be patronised? Little Goody-Two-Shoes doesn't like being patronised and neither do I.

So who are we going to talk about then? Well anyone but me. Show me someone else's life where they have seen unimaginable things and regularly do crazy things and I will talk to you about their messed up lives and messed up behaviour. Hell, I might even tell you what they need to do to sort out their lives. I might not always see it immediately, but

> Talk about others, out comes the social microscope and discussion. Talk about me and the microscope is shoved aside and silence prevails.

with your guidance I will come to see the lack of normality in another person's life.

You see, everyone loves to talk about other people, to judge their behaviour, their actions, to analyse them to a much higher degree than they would ever do to themselves. Look at the amount of people chatting about the latest reality TV show, giving their ten cents worth. Talk about others, out comes the social microscope and discussion. Talk about me and the microscope is shoved aside and silence prevails.

You get me talking about others by showing me films, TV programmes, anything where there are parallels between my life and the lives of the people in the films. You'll probably find that I've watched half these films already because I've needed to so that I can point at them and say-'Look, that's the same as me. It's totally normal'. But if you watch them with me and discuss what is going on, we un-normalise the behaviour for the people in the films, and consequently hopefully un-normalise the behaviour for me.

Over time I may start to make the parallels between their lives and mine. I will gradually over time, think through my perception of my life and bit by bit alter those perceptions to something nearing reality. And as I do so, the pan of inner turmoil will go from a raging boil to a simmer, until hopefully one day I will just stop boiling all together. The inner conflict will be gone- my view of my life will be at one with my deep down subconscious understanding of how it should be.

I might do this completely for myself or I might need some gentle encouragement or steering from you. But whatever you do, do not tell me outright that my life and behaviour is not normal. Take me to the edge, but that is all you can do. I have to discover this for myself.

By doing it this way, starting with others then moving on to me, by taking it slow, you give me time to form new perceptions of my life, and therefore give me time to reform my identity. Tell me outright that my life, and by association that I am not normal, then you kneecap me; I fall to the ground. Give me time and encouragement and I will still be able to stand as I rebuild myself. It is generally less messy that way; it involves less kickback from me- less abuse, less violence, less police.

So in short, looking at others, helps me look at me. Seeing their mess helps me see my mess and helps me to hope and yearn for more in my life. My definition of 'normal' changes, but my desire to be 'normal' does not. And so the behavioural and life changes begin. I'm beginning to walk, you've just got to help me.

GUIDANCE

BY MY SIDE

It's just me. Just me, on my own trying to work out how to do this thing called life. And well I'm not very good at it mostly. Neither are most of the people around me. So you could say I'm a bit clueless. A leaky boat, cast adrift, praying that the next wave that comes crashing down doesn't sink me.

Even the people who try to help me often don't really help. They try and take over, try and tell me what to do. They try and climb aboard and declare themselves the captain and issue orders as to what I need to do to get myself seaworthy. Would be nice to be asked. Then I could tell them that I don't want them to take over- it's my life. As it is, I often end up throwing them overboard anyhow. I'd rather be stuck on a sinking ship that's mine, than a fixed-up boat that's not. Either way, I still end up alone.

Even if they try and patch up the holes and the leaks, they won't fix the problem. If they don't draw alongside me, find out what the fabric of my life is, how I tick, what motivates me, the structure of my vessel, then they won't be able to find the right sort of materials to make me watertight. They'll just apply some generic 'fixing' material that won't bond, won't become an integral part of my vessel, of me. And over time I'll start to leak again and the patch will fall off. I'll be as leaky as I ever was.

The truth is that no-one can fix me and my life while I passively sit here, having a makeover done to me. I need to be involved. Whose boat is this anyway? By all means, guide me towards the location of my leaks, help me explore why I might need to apply some patches, show me what sort of patches I can try, and involve me in the sourcing of any services or materials I might need. If I have no clue how to do it, show me. Don't do it for me, show me and help me to learn how to do it.

No-one can fix my life while I passively sit here— I need to be involved.

I need people to come alongside me and guide me as I fill out things like job or benefit applications. Show me how to access help and support from charities and council services. Show me where to go and who to ask. And if I lack the skills to do any of this, like the literacy skills to fill out a form or the communications skills to state my needs or ask for help, assist me to gain the skills so I can. Yes, I will need greater support while I gain these skills, but still involve me in the process so I at least learn how to do it in the meantime. Just don't do it all for me. Help me to do it for myself.

This way I'll own the repairs. The repairs will bond as the solutions chosen by me will match my individual structure the best way possible. And as I will have chosen them for myself and I will have invested my time and effort into achieving them, with your help, they will be way more likely to last in the long-term.

And you know what else? The next time I spring a leak I'll have a better idea of what to do, even if I don't have you to call on. You'll have given me a toolkit, not a patch.

So it's about you drawing alongside me and showing me the way. I have to steer and do the repairs. You are at most my navigator, pointing me in the right direction, but I always have the option of going my own way. If you respectfully draw alongside me rather than gung-ho climbing aboard and imposing yourself as the captain, I'll respect you back and will listen.

And the biggest lesson for me from all of this? It's not the new tools that I've now got (although they are awesome and will last me a lifetime). It's that I am capable. I'm not totally useless. I can actually do stuff. I'll have begun to beat the demons that keep me down, keep me doing nothing cos I think I don't have the ability to change. Self-efficacy I think they call it. Each time I hit a storm or spring a leak, instead of cowering in fear below deck, I'll face the problem, whip out my toolkit and use my new tools. And every time I use them I'll get better and better at using them.

You just have to first show me that the tools exist and show me when and how to use them. The second time you might only need to remind me I've got them. Eventually I'll use them without even having to think too hard. It will have become a part of my structure, the way I deal with life. I will have learned how to navigate rather than hide from the storms of life. I will sail under the flag of resilience.

And even if I don't turn to ask you cos I already know what to do, or because you're not involved in my life anymore, I'll still feel you there beside me. I won't feel so alone and helpless anymore. People who have been by my side and have given me the tools to live aren't easily forgotten. Your patience, your compassion and your guidance will always remain even if not your name or face. You will always be there beside me, even if it is just the tiniest whisper in the wind as I set out to sail each day.

NEEDS IDENTIFICATION

MY STICKY TAPE:
YOU CAN'T TAKE AWAY WITHOUT
REPLACING

I am stuck together with sticky tape. Not your good quality Sellotape or Scotch Tape mind, the cheap stuff that only works some of the time. Put it this way, if I get caught in a shower I'm in big trouble.

So trying to get me to change my life or even little bits of my life is no easy ask. All the pieces interweave and 'inter-stick' and if you mess with one, you affect the other pieces. Plus if you rip a piece off I will have a big gaping hole, which can be a bit draughty and can have bad effects on my structural soundness. So I will obviously try to stuff the hole in whatever way I can, to keep myself together.

So if you try to help me take away one of my pieces of tape, one of the parts of my life, be it membership of a gang, excessive drinking, drug use, violence, self-harm you have to think about what I will fill that draughty hole with. That bit of tape was put there for a reason in the first place; it met a deep need. So you can't go ripping it off without thinking about how I will meet that need in another more positive way. If you do just go ahead and rip it off then I will either eventually find the exact same bit of tape and stick it back on or I will find another equally useless unhelpful piece of tape to cover the gap. Nobody can stand a draught, you get me?

Instead, you need to explore that hole that the tape covers and find the best material to fill the hole with, some super-duper super-insulatory material that will feel way better than the crappy old tape used to. Something that will keep the draught out, something that will last and has real structural integrity, will keep me really warm and stable inside, something that will beat the old tape, hands down.

So if my 'gang tape' gives me a sense of belonging, gives me a family, then before you can even get me to consider giving that up, you have to help me see that there are better groups and 'families' to belong to, groups that need me, groups that will feel like family and don't bully me into doing stuff that I really deep down don't want to do. Groups where what I do isn't motivated by fear. Groups where I can get rid of my stress and aggression without a 10 year sentence tag. One idea would be to get me playing in a sports team. That would do all of that and is worth a think.

Or if my 'drink and drugs tape' or 'self-harm tape' is helping me to block out or just cope with feelings, real bad feelings of what has happened to me and how I've been treated, you have to help me get to a point where I don't feel the need to block out those feelings, where I can accept those feelings and move on, rather than being held prisoner by them. So you need to replace my tape with better, more positive coping strategies. You need to supply me with a kick-ass toolkit of strategies.

Or if I'm antsy and can blow up in an explosion of anger dead easy, you could explore the needs I am trying to meet that underlie my anger and find alternative ways of getting those needs met. It might be that I get well peeved when people don't listen to what I'm saying. So it's about me looking at why people might not be listening and coming up with strategies to help people to listen to me, like choosing my moments, my words, and body movements and expressing my frustrations in a calmer, assertive way. At the same time I also need to be dealing with the fact that I do seem to be a tightly wound person and finding ways to release some of that tension through sport or music or whatever works for me. It's another situation where that kick-ass strategies toolkit is needed to replace my 'anger tape'.

Or it might be that I'm not actually angry at the people I explode at, but that I'm angry about the way no-one seems to give a crap about me and I deliberately push people away with my explosions cos I'm scared they're going to reject me like everyone else. In which case getting rid of my anger tape may involve

Identify the need the tape fulfills, then remove and replace.

bringing someone into my life, either currently known or new, like a mentor, who can take some time and care. That might even be you. The tape was covering my need to be cared for and fear of rejection and if you can replace that with some solid unconditional care then I won't need that tape anymore.

It's simple really. You can't take away without replacing. And the replacement needs to be good, needs to address my underlying need for me to even consider it.

I'm not saying that I'll be falling over myself to do the swap, even if it does seem quite good. Any change is risky. Quite often there will be some messy negative fall-out from making the change, so it can't be taken lightly. But if you help me to see that in the long-run life will be better, that I will be better held together than these pieces of tape currently manage, then I might be prepared to take the risk of a small step, a little pull of the tape. I might then gain the courage to keep on pulling and to make the replacement. But it just ain't gonna happen if there is no half-decent alternative and for that I need you to take the time to understand me, to come up with some interesting ideas and for you to encourage me to make the change. I need you to help me see the possibility of a more solid, stable me that doesn't need to rely on tape.

FORWARD THINKING

DON'T LET ME DEFINE MYSELF BY MY PAST

I am more than my past; more than the things that people have done to me, more than the things that I have done to others. Yet just as others find it hard to understand this, so do I.

I live in a mental space where my reality, my sense of truth about the world and myself is formed by what people have told me or done to me, and a lot of it isn't very nice. Sometimes people say what they say because of their own problems, sometimes it's in response to my behaviour, and often it's a combination of the two. But the end result is still the same. I get beaten down by words and actions and then slowly but surely I end up defining myself in those terms, and keep myself down, stuck in a never-ending negative view of myself.

So I end up thinking that I'm worthless, that no-one cares

and that there is nothing I can do to make myself feel better or to change my lot in life. I'm just a dreg and will always be just a dreg. I tell myself every day that I just have to accept that and carry on as I am. That is how I survive. If I don't wish for better then I don't end up being disappointed. And believe me, I can't take any more disappointment in life. So I just try and survive as I am, it's the safest thing.

So I end up living in a whirling pot of negativity, of closed doors, of hurt... and it never stops... unless you help me break out of it. I need you to give me hope, to give me a sense of possibility, a taste of what life could be. I need you to show me that life isn't just something that is done to me. Show me that I can reclaim my life and can be in control. I need to see that things can be different, change *can* happen.

Yes, life has been crap. People have neglected me, abused me, generally not met my basic human need for love, for care, for support. Often a large part of why I am the way I am today is other people's fault. But don't let me stop there, in just blaming. If you do I will be no nearer to solving the problem that is my life. I will still be stuck in my pot of negativity and hurt, dwelling on the past and thinking that nothing can change.

Show me that my power and control lies in how I respond to my past. Only I can choose how I respond and that is my power. Whether I'm still around those that mistreat me or not, whether you are in the process of removing me from that situation or not, show me how their treatment of me is not who I am and does not have to define my life. Show me alternate ways of validating myself and getting a sense of value and self-worth. Help me to move on from blame to finding solutions to my problems.

Life then doesn't look so gloomy. I suddenly have choices to make; I'm back in the driving seat of my life.

One of the best ways you can help me achieve this is to help me set goals for my life. Goals are all about the future, about looking forward, about possibility, about change that I control, everything that I need right now.

But how do you get me to this alien place of goal-setting? I'm so stuck in surviving now, I don't know how to do anything else.

THE GOAL-SETTING PATH

Teach me to dream

So much of my life has been about being stuck. About being stuck in the past and not being able to see a way out. About listening to negative voices that have crushed me, told me that I'm worthless, causing me to be stuck listening to a track on loop telling me how I don't deserve anything good. Or a track saying that my dreams are unrealistic, that I'm not smart enough or good enough. Or stuck with the track that tells me that because of what I've experienced, I'm dirty or tarnished or stupid, that there's something wrong with me, that because of this I can't possibly make anything of my life.

My negative view of myself may have developed at such a young age that I've forgotten how to dream. Or I still dream, but feel guilty about it, stupid about it, so I shut it down before my dreams fully form and can be grasped. Or the dreaming itself contributes to my depressed view of life, because they just highlight for me what I can't become.

So you need to provide me with a safe supportive space where I can explore dreams I may have had in my past that I've suppressed. A space where I can explore new ones. You might need to feed me with ideas, with examples from your own life. And you need me to know that there is no such thing as a silly dream. Even if it is fantastical like wanting to be a bird, there may be nuggets of what I actually want for myself in reality in there if you help me explore. It might be that it's the being outside, the total freedom, and being in nature that appeals.

Encourage me to just sit and be quiet and let my mind wander and see what materialises. Tell me to write or draw about my dreams in addition to discussing them with you.

Or complete one of the following exercises:

1. *The Perfect Day*

Imagine the best day of your life. Who do you spend time with? What are you doing? What enables you to do this?

2. *The Awesome List*

Write out a no-holds barred list of what your life would look like if it was completely awesome.

Setting goals to help me realise my dreams

Once I know what my dreams are, then I need to be helped to set the goals, the concrete steps that I need to take in order to make my dreams a reality.

A central part of this is seeing what the difference is

between now and where I want to be, because that is the ground that needs to be covered. It's about identifying the barriers that currently exist that stop me from getting there, and working out what needs to be done so I can overcome them.

So I might have dreamt that I am surrounded by people who care for me. Maybe I've dreamt of having a family one day and of going to the beach together. Maybe I have dreamt this because I don't get this from my own parents- Dad is AWOL and Mum isn't coping on her own and drinks too much. The message I get is that my parents didn't give a stuff about me.

From this we work out that I want to be with people who care for me, so that is my **headline goal**. The barrier I have is that no one is providing that for me now in the usual places you would find this- at home. So now we need to consider how to overcome that barrier. So we start to problem solve together, to think about whether there are other members of the family who can provide that for me, or maybe I'd really benefit from a mentor who can be that person for me, or maybe joining a sports team would surround me with people who care as we all look out for each other. We are then setting our **sub-goals**, the actual practical things needed to meet the headline goal. We can also be working on improving things with Mum at the same time, another sub-goal. If things change with Mum then great, if they don't then at least I am meeting my need elsewhere. I am choosing to own and carry on with my life and refuse to be held captive by other people's inadequacies.

Once we have the headline goals and the sub-goals, we can then work on the **stepping-stone goals**, the shorter-term practical things that we need to do to meet the higher level goals. These are the things that I need to do in the next weeks or months.

So after discussion we might decide that my headline goal of wanting to be cared for, should have the sub-goals of meeting with a mentor, and joining the local basketball team. You, as my worker, have the sub-goals of working with Mum to help her cope better, and obviously helping me meet my sub-goals. The stepping stone goals are then where we seriously drill down into what we need to do and these should always be SMART and should always be written down.

S: Specific- *what exactly will I achieve?*

M: Measurable- *how will I know when I have reached this goal?*

A: Achievable- *is achieving this goal realistic with effort and commitment?*

R: Relevant- *why is this goal significant to my life?*

T: Time-bound- *when will I achieve this goal?*

So for the sub-step, 'joining the local basketball team', one of the SMART stepping-stone goals could be:

In the next two weeks (Time-bound), I will attend (Specific-not demanding participation which might be the next stepping-stone goal) the basketball club at least once (Measurable and Achievable as not asking too much). This is so I can make friends in a team, have fun together and get to the point where we might all look out for each other (Relevant).

Reviewing goals

After the time specified in the stepping-stone goal, we can

then review my progress. If the goals have been well planned for me, I will hopefully have achieved them. If not, we can reset more achievable ones, or maybe try again. The key thing is to aim for success, and this might mean setting what seems like the tiniest of goals for you. Remember, I'm trying to get used to doing things differently and trying to believe that what you say is true- I can change and I can feel differently about myself.

And it's not about rushing me either (see the chapter on 'Patience'). It's all about helping me move forward, bit by bit at a rate suitable for me. Remember it was the tortoise that won the race; slowly but surely.

So if I didn't meet my basketball attendance goal, maybe we need to rework that one to:

In the next two weeks, I will go with [name of worker] to watch a basketball club training session from the sidelines, at least once. This is so I can see how a team works together and are friends, how they have fun together and they all look out for each other.

It might be that going to watch turns into joining in, in which case great, but the point is that the achievability of the goal, particularly in the beginning, is as great as it possibly can be. And why? Because each time I achieve a goal, I believe in my ability to change things that little bit more. And every time I achieve a stepping-stone goal, I can see that I am moving ever closer to achieving my overall headline goal and that my dreams aren't nonsense, that they are achievable and that I can get myself there. I am making progress rather than being stuck in the here and now, frozen because I can't stop dwelling on and being defined by the past.

Over time the direction of my goals might change as I come to know myself more, me as defined by me, rather than me solely defined by my past or by others. So in the example of feeling cared for, the goals may change and new ones will be added as time goes on. It becomes an evolving plan, just as my life is. The important thing is that the goals keep on moving me forwards.

Sometimes my dream and headline goal might seem fantastical and unachievable, but please let me dream. If that is where I want to go, help me head off forwards in that direction, it is better than going nowhere, constantly looking back over my shoulder. In the process of making and achieving my stepping-stone goals, I may well formulate a new destination headline goal, or dream a new dream that comes about precisely because I have been growing as a person, finding out about myself and my strengths and capabilities through those stepping-stone goals. So please don't discard my dreams as ridiculous, because that ridiculousness may well be the one thing that motivates me to move forwards.

FORWARD NOT BACK

I then become all about where I am going, and less about where I have been, what I have done and what people have said about me. I stop looking back at my past all the time and start to look forward to my future, feeling that I am in control of my life and where it is going.

Whatever my issues, I need to be able to look forward, at new possibilities rather than just dwelling on old hurts and pains. Yes I do need to work through my past but don't leave me there. Help me see who I can be, rather than who I was or was made out to be in the past. Help me regain control of my life and see that it is me who holds the key that can let me out of my prison. I may not have built the walls but I can break out. You just need to show me how.

MUTUAL LEARNING, MUTUAL RESPECT

This may come as a shock, but you don't know everything. It will undoubtedly come as a shock to most teens that they don't know everything too. How many times have we heard the old rhetorical when speaking to teens about something that they don't want to talk about, "What do you know?".

Yes, as an adult you generally have the trump card on knowledge by virtue of your years, but the number of candles on your birthday cake does not mean you are the authority on every aspect of life (even if you may be the authority on how to put out a small fire). So when engaging in a conversation with a teenager enter it in the expectation that you might learn something from them. This is the breeding ground of genuine respect- it shows you value their input and they are more likely to value yours. This is worth its weight in gold when you are trying to change someone's behaviour for the better.

And it's not just about finding about them, which they will expect you to be doing in your sessions, like asking questions about school. It's the sharing of knowledge separate from themselves and their lives, shared by them with you, that can change the dynamic of your relationship with them.

For example, one young person I worked with was doing a vocational qualification in gardening at his Pupil Referral Unit (where kids in the UK go who have been permanently excluded from school). Being a bit of a gardener myself I made a point of asking him for tips, like how to stop slugs eating my lettuces without having to spend a fortune on slug pellets. He was genuinely thrilled to tell me to use crushed eggshells around my lettuces.

Asking them about something they know about gives them a real sense of worth and boosts their self-esteem no end. The bonus here was that it motivated him even more to continue attending the PRU and to get a qualification. From then on he really started to engage with me and he

If you value my input, I'll be more likely to value yours.

really turned his life around all because he started to trust me and he started to believe in himself. It all started with slugs and lettuces!

I have even be known to ask questions of young people that has them rolling their eyes and giggling because to them I am asking the dumbest question in the world. Back in the (olden!) days when textspeak was in its infancy I actually asked a girl what 'lol' meant. She nearly died from laughter, but she did tell me. It makes me laugh even thinking about it now, but by me asking her, I showed her that there is no such thing as a dumb question. This is role-modelling in a very simple but effective way.

By asking 'dumb' questions we show them that if they have something they want to know but feel stupid asking about, that they should just go right ahead and ask. Learning something is never stupid.

So in your sessions make space mentally and time practically to learn something from your young person. In so doing, you give them a voice and some sense of worth. It's priceless.

COURAGE

DID YOU KNOCK ON MY DOOR?

Did you knock on my door? Did you want to see? Or was the sterile incomplete description in my report enough for you? Or what your colleague told you over the kettle? Or what my social worker told you over the phone?

You want to see what my life is like. You ask me in your appointment room, in the cafe or in detention, to tell you what life at home is like. But why should I bother to tell you? Do you really want to see? Your words tell me you don't cos if you really wanted to know, you wouldn't ask, you'd come.

Even if I try and tell you without you coming to look, you wouldn't get to see it all. You'd be seeing it only through my eyes. You wouldn't find out about the things that I don't even notice any more and wouldn't think to mention.

The abnormal that has become my normal. The holes in the

walls and the doors that tell of anger, the smell of alcohol and weed that clings to the curtains, the rubbish strewn everywhere. Or my Mum and Dad at the door, determined not to let you in. Or the grubby little sister with the matted hair and the rotten teeth. Or my Mum on her own, full of care and concern but struggling to manage life, let alone me. Or the foster carer who gives me a roof but clearly no more.

Or you might see a well-kept home or a home with more luxuries than our family income should allow. You might see a mantelpiece with pictures of everyone but me, or a photo of someone that died that I can't bear to mention. Or an almost forgotten sibling whose name is never voiced, cos he's doing time.

You might see some people pop round- the regular visit of the well-known offender or the group of older kids that hang around right outside my door. Or you might just see that my home life seems pretty 'normal'. Either way, there's so much to see.

Visual clues are everything and if you limit those clues to just looking at me, you are never going to really see me, my life, my family, my circumstances. The visual provides no place to hide- it provides prompts to conversations, it opens the eyes of your heart and leads you to ask the right questions, to begin to 'get' me and why I do what I do. Like who  might be influencing me, who might be ignoring me, who frightens me or annoys me. The stuff of relationships, the stuff of my life.

In some ways I 'get' that you probably don't particularly want to come and see my life in its rawness, particularly if it's dirty and it's smelly. Which is all the more reason to do it. It shows me you care, that you are interested in me, that you care enough to see beyond the dirt- you really want to connect with me. You'll experience discomfort in your pursuit of my happiness.

I know the voice in your head- *'I'm not going to that God-forsaken place if I don't have to!'*. Well I'm glad you have that choice, I don't. This is where I live. If you care, you'll come.

'I'm too busy. I just don't have the time'. Please don't kid yourself. You'll learn more about me and connect with me (and with my parents and carers) more in one home visit than you could in ten times as many conversations in your cosy world. And connection means everything to me. Yes it requires more effort from you, but the benefits far outweigh the cost. If you really want to see me and help me, this you have to do.

I get it, you're scared. You don't know what you will find- 'normal life' or uncomfortable hell, and what do you do if you see things you don't want to see? You're tired, you're overworked, you don't have the energy to deal with what might be behind the door and the emotional response you might have. So you roll down the shutters and you don't come. And you wonder why I don't engage with you? It's because you didn't engage with me and my life.

It's the fear of the unknown. It can haunt you as much as it haunts me. I'm scared to make changes in my life cos I don't know what they'll look like, whether I can do it, whether I have the strength. And if you want me to pluck up the courage to give it a go, then you need to show me what doing something different, something out of the ordinary looks like. Show me how brave and deep our internal strength can be. Show me what courage looks like. Knock on my door.

You'll learn that things aren't as scary as they seem, that being afraid of the unknown is scarier than giving it a go and knowing. That the street that I live on is not going to pounce and devour you like you think it will, that the sofa you sit on is not going to eat you, that most doors are opened rather than slammed in your face.

You'll see the humanity rather than the scare stories, the people amidst the hardship. So the outcome is usually better than expected and even when it is worse, you'll know you did the right thing. You reached out. You tried to connect with me, with my life.

We've both just got to face the unknown and make it known, remove the debilitating fear that prevents us from pushing ourselves forwards, from connecting, from changing. We're more alike than you realise, you and me.

You're the adult, not me, so I ask that you take the first step and show me the way to overcome the fear of the unknown. You lead and I'll be more likely to follow. Just knock on my door and I'll show you my life.

Please note:

In a very small number of cases it is genuinely unsafe to

make home visits to some young people due to issues such as dangerous dogs, previous violence towards professionals or because it is a drug den. If in doubt, consult your line manager.

In these cases you clearly can't knock on their own personal front door. In which case, knock on the front door of their community- meet the young person somewhere in their community, like a café, diner or in the park. Just reach out to them, where they live, in whatever way you can.

And as a matter of course with all out-of-office visits, if there is not an automated system in place, always make sure that someone knows where you are and when you are expected to be finished, and call them when you are done. This is belt-and-braces keeping yourself safe, but please don't let it perturb and prevent you from knocking the door in the first place.

NON-JUDGEMENTALISM

START WITH ME WHERE I AM

Oh would you just shut up? Please, I beg you. *'You must change.... You must do this, you must do that..... You'll end up in prison... You'll end up with no qualifications.... You won't be able to get a job.... You'll end up addicted....'* Good God, put away your defective crystal ball would you? What the hell do you know about me? I've got a handle on this, I know what I'm doing. The only person with a problem here is you- you and your relentless interfering. Let me live my life the way I want to, it's going just fine without your judgement and comments.

So I'm entrenched. I'm determined about my rightness and your complete wrongness. So before we've even started discussing something, we've stopped. No communication has gone down. I think you're a tool who isn't worth listening to. You think I'm a clueless immature naive inexperienced idiot who is clearly going to learn the hard way.

There is only one piece of learning that occurs through these sorts of interaction- how to be as stubborn as a mule. Nothing gets a teen to the heights of stubbornness faster than being told what to do.

Surely there's a better way. There *has* to be a better way. What would be less irritating? What would stop the shutters going down? What would keep the lines of communication open and the possibility of something different, alive?

WHERE IS MY HEAD AT?

Whether you've known me for years or have only just met me, start as if you do not know me. Cos even if you have known me since I was knee-high to a grasshopper, chances are you do not know what is going on in my head right now. And even if you have read a doorstop of a file on me, you do not know me as I experience me. All you have read is other people's experiences of me. While this can be informative as background information, at the end of the day, it is you talking or working with me, not them, so you need to find out about me, from me.

So to understand how I tick, you need to listen, to ask questions and listen. And you know what you have to leave out if you really want to get to know me? The judgements, the condescension, any side comments like, *'well that was a bit stupid'* because as soon as you do, the shutters will lower a little. With each new comment or suggestion of what I should or must do, the shutters lower further, until the light is shut out entirely.

So if you want to find out why I'm bunking off school, you don't start by saying, *"Why on earth are you not going to school? That's ridiculous, you need your education"*. You just ask the question, *"So what's all this bunking off school about?"*. You may well get a "dunno" from me, but instead of you seeing this as your opportunity to launch into a lecture as to why I shouldn't be doing it, you ask more questions or express why you are concerned: *"I'm just asking because I'm worried about you."*

The key thing in all of this is that you are respecting where I am in the process of thinking about changing my behaviour. Often I will not have even contemplated doing anything differently. So if you then launch into discussing with me how I should change my behaviour, like why I should be going to school, you have a) already left me behind, and b) demonstrated that you have no idea of what is going on in my head and my life. All you then do is confirm for me how clueless you are, and how there is really no point listening to you. Heels dug in, behaviour unchanged.

You have to do the groundwork first, no advice or comments attached, to find out where I am in the process of change so that you can pitch what you are saying correctly.

THE STAGES OF CHANGE MODEL

While you might think that change is like an on-off switch- we're either doing it or we're not, it is actually more complicated than that. If we pick apart the process of making a change, it is the mental stages, processes and actions that any person needs to go through,

1) before making a change,

2) while making a change, and

3) while sticking with (maintaining) that change.

Prochaska and DeClemente's (1983) model of the stages of change shows the thinking and action processes that a person will go through on the way to changing their behaviour and sticking to that new behaviour.

In the process of change a person moves from being uninterested, unaware or unwilling to make a change (precontemplation), to considering a change (contemplation), to deciding and preparing to make a change. Genuine, determined action is then taken and, over time, they attempt to keep up (maintain) the new behaviour.

Making mistakes and falling back into old habits (relapses) are almost inevitable and become part of the process of working towards changes that stick (lifelong change). When we stick with our new behaviour for a long time and it becomes our new 'normal', the model says we have successfully made the change, so we exit the cycle. Some never fully reach this stage as they feel that there is always some potential for relapse and they constantly have to actively think about and consciously decide to stick with their new behaviour (maintenance).

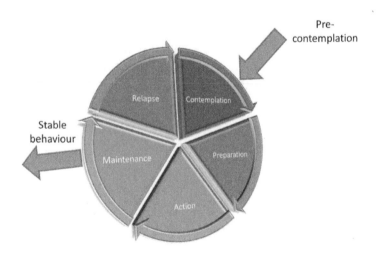

But what do these stages look like in reality when working with me? What's the practical flesh on the these technical bones?

If I'm at the **pre-contemplation stage**, I am not even considering changing. I'm usually thinking one of three things.

1. Life is just fine as it is, my behaviour isn't a problem.
2. I've tried changing my behaviour before and it didn't work, so trying to change is pointless. It's not even worth considering.
3. What I'm doing is perfectly normal. It hasn't even occurred to me that there is a different way of behaving.

Most of the time, teens like me who are difficult to engage, are at this pre-contemplation stage. A large part of what your work with me is going to involve is getting me from this stage to the contemplation stage.

During the **contemplation stage**, I've entertained the idea of changing but I'm really not sure whether I want to or not; I'm ambivalent. My behaviour as it is, probably has some benefits, like the fact that bunking off school with my friends is a lot more fun than having to work and being told what to do in school. So even though I may now be aware that I am damaging my chances of leaving school with good grades and that I could gain the opportunity to go to college or get a decent job by getting back in school, I am having to grapple with a sense of loss of the benefits of my current behaviour. I'm going through the mental process of weighing up the losses and gains of making the change. Common barriers to making a change include time, expense, effort/ hassle, fear, perceptions of inadequacy.

At the **preparation stage**, I have decided I want to make the change so I start to think about how I am going to make this happen. So if I decide I want to stop bunking off, I need to start thinking through practical strategies of how I'm going to overcome the pull to continue in my old behaviour. How am I going to tell my friends I'm not bunking off with them? How am I going to cope with this? Learning and practising assertiveness skills, positive self-talk and stress-reduction techniques would come into play here. If I have been bunking off due to difficulties accessing the work as a result of being dyslexic, having ADHD or autism, for example (whether formally diagnosed or not), then I will need strategies to help me access that work and to increase the understanding of my difficulties amongst the staff in school.

The **action stage** is exactly what it says. It's when I start to make the change.

Maintenance and relapse prevention is then the big thing. I've started to make the change, but sticking to it is now the big challenge so that my change in behaviour can become permanent.

I will inevitably fall off my change wagon at times. Sometimes this may stop the whole change process as I decide to give up entirely. Sometimes I may need to recycle through the stages of change in order to decide whether I want to try again. I might enter the pre-contemplation phase again. Or I might re-enter at the contemplation stage, revisiting why I decided to make the change in the first place to be re-motivated, to re-prepare and to try again.

Can you now see why it's so important that before you do anything else, you work out where I am on this cycle of change? It's so important because it affects the kind of stuff you will explore and talk about with me and ultimately whether I think you are clueless or not. My disengagement is often not so much to do with me, but that you've failed to engage me because what you've been saying hasn't been relevant.

The problem for you is that often when I am in the pre-contemplation stage I am an extremely difficult character to talk to. I may infuriate you to the point where you end up falling into the trap of arguing with me, effectively telling me that what I think is wrong or that I am misguided. Even if you are the most patient character who has the kindest voice and tone imaginable and you say, *"I'm not sure you are making the best choices, why don't you try this?"*, you are still going to cause the shutters to fall. While you might just get lip-service from me rather than an outright, *'f*** off you idiot'* from me, the underlying view of you is the same. You're clueless and know nothing about me. You are not starting with me from where I am, you are starting with me from where you want me to be.

Making the leap from pre-contemplative to contemplative is one of the biggest leaps I will take, and one of the hardest for you to help me make. And you can't rush it. It will take as long as it takes. It's while trying to make this leap that a lot of young people like me get left behind. Workers give up. They are in too much of a hurry to get me to the contemplative stage, they start telling me how their way is so much better than my current way before I've even decided what I'm currently doing is even a problem or that I could be doing life any differently.

So what can you do to help me make that leap? How do you avoid falling into the trap of arguing with me at worst and making me dig my heels in, or giving me advice that I never asked for in the first place and causing me to switch off?

DEALING WITH RESISTANCE TALK

When I tell you that there is nothing wrong with my behaviour, or that I don't care, it can seem like an almost impossible task for you to avoid lecturing me. You've got to correct me, haven't you? Well no, you don't actually. In fact, not responding and ensuring you do not end up in a debate with me is just about the most important thing you can do. Why? Because a debate (or argument as they often end up being) creates an

environment where I can finely hone my arguments for not changing, my resistance talk. What you need to be doing is getting me to explore the idea of change, and increasing my change talk.

Resistance talk includes:

- Statements that deny there is an issue to be dealt with:

    'Get lost, I don't have a problem with my friends'

    'Everyone else my age is taking drugs. What's the problem?'

- Statements about intentions not to change:

'If you think I'm going to listen to anything you've got to say then you are mad. I'm fine as I am thanks. It's you with the problem.'

- Statements about the advantages of the status quo:

  'If I don't go to college I'm way more chilled out.'

  'People know just to back off and leave me alone.'

  'I go my own way, no one can stop me.'

  'It's buzzin', pure buzzin''

- Statements about the disadvantages of change:

  'If I don't smoke I get totally stressed out. I can't sleep, can't do nothing.'

  'If I tell them I'm not doing it anymore, everyone will think I've gone soft, a total pussy'.

  'What am I supposed to do on the weekends if I stop drinking? Might as well die, life would be so boring.'

- Statements of pessimism about change:

  'What's the point anyway? It'll make sod all difference to anything'

  'I can't change. It's just the way I am.'

- Non-engagement:

  'Whatever'

  'Huh?'

Silence, or change of subject.

Don't just take my word for it, research has shown that with young people the clearest indicator of change is a reduction in this kind of resistance talk (Bauer et al 2008). So it's vital we don't debate. It's counter-productive. It makes me less likely to change, not more.

You see, arguing with adults is a normal part of my teen developmental process. Developing a greater sense of independence is an important part of my route to adulthood and greater resistance to adult authority is a part of this process. When an adult tries to tell or even persuade me why I need to change, I just see them trying to limit my personal freedoms (and my drive towards greater independence and adulthood) and so I'm more likely to have a negative response and to engage in resistance talk (Brehm 1966).

So if you can't argue the case for change, what *can* you do? There's nothing left is there? I need to see the other side of the debate and because I'm stuck in my own rigid thinking, you're thinking, who's going to show it to me? Well the answer is actually no-one. It's not going to be shown to me. I, in my autonomous drive am going to find it for myself with your help.

Your job is not to tell me what I should do, it is to help me argue my own case for change.

Your job is not to tell me what I should do, it is to help me argue my own case for change.

HELP ME MAKE MY OWN CASE FOR CHANGE

So how do you help me to argue my own case for change? How do you get round all the objections, the arguments, the resistance talk, the sheer bloody-minded opposition?

Put me in the driving seat

When beginning to try to get me to reconsider a behaviour, if you start off with a statement that shows that you realise that I am in control of what I do and the decisions I make, and not you, then my ears will prick up. Trust me, us teens don't hear this often from adults, if ever, so it really does make us take notice. We are far more used to being told how what we are doing is wrong and what we should be doing instead.

Once you've made it clear that we are in control, that we have this thing called autonomy, you can then explain how our interactions are going to work: *'I want to help you make the best decisions for you. I don't want to lay down the law, I don't want to tell you what to do. I just want to help you explore what's going on in your life at the moment and to really understand where you are coming from. I really want to explore together and understand you more so I can help you decide how you want to handle this situation.'*

It then becomes really hard for me to argue with you. If someone tells us that they actually want to listen to me, that they respect my right to choose, there is nothing left for me to fight against. I might still be really suspicious of you, and will throw out resistance talk and continue to avoid addressing the issue. A classic would be, *'There is no poxy situation. Just get lost'*. In which case, you will need to use one of the other following strategies.

Get me to tell you how I see the situation

Whatever you do, don't tell me what you see the situation as being, e.g. drinking too much, being too aggressive etc. Even if it is well meant and framed helpfully like, *'I really want to help you with your over-drinking'* or *'I really want to understand why you get so angry that you lose control so I can help you'*, all I will hear is that you are more interested in your own take on things than you are on listening to my take on things. I'll just end up trying to avoid listening to you, will dig in my heels and will resistance-talk till the cows come home to avoid having to engage with you.

If you tell me how you view the situation you are also missing out on an opportunity to understand how I view my behaviour. You will miss pointers as to how much and what sort of work you need to do with me to get me to a place where I will contemplate change.

A straightforward way of getting me to tell you how I see the situation is to ask an open-ended question about why I think I am having this conversation or are in this session with you: *'Why do you think you are here?'* (If you have experienced further resistance as highlighted above, moving the conversation onto this question could be a way of moving the conversation on).

For example, with anger control issues, you might get the following answers and these will give you some indicator of my readiness for change:

- *'because you think I need anger management?'*

[I probably don't really think I have a problem, or if I do have some realisation I clearly don't think it is as big a problem as you do. Some way to go before ready to make a change.]

- *'because the court said I had to'*

[I'm not really interested in change, I'm just here through coercion.]

- *'because I've got a temper'*

[I'm possibly open to the idea of changing my behaviour as I'm owning it.]

- *'I have no idea'*

[I may just be nervous, may not be interested in engaging, or have no idea that my behaviour is a problem and so nowhere near making a change.]

One simple question like this can allow me to express myself and provide you with valuable information as to what I see the issues as being and how resistant to change I really am. Most importantly you avoid creating an environment where I get to do what I often like to do- argue. If you don't put words in my mouth then there is nothing for me to argue against and I don't get to wheel out all my usual resistance talk.

Avoid using the term 'problem'

Don't refer to my situation or the issues in my life as 'problems'. This just comes across as judgemental. If I think you are judging me then I am way more likely to clam up or to engage in resistance talk, arguing why I do not have a problem. Terms like 'situation', or 'issue' come across much better.

RESPONDING TO RESISTANCE TALK

Even using all these techniques, it's almost guaranteed that I will engage in resistance talk at some point along the way. So what do you do? How do you avoid getting into a debate with me?

Neutrality and rolling with resistance

Have you ever tried to argue with someone who refuses to argue with you? Have you ever tried to argue with someone who is really listening to you and trying to understand a situation from your perspective? It's virtually impossible.

So when I throw out resistance talk to try and get you to argue with me or to make you go away, disarm me by refusing to argue or debate with me. Go Swiss and take a neutral position.

This way you don't end up going down a conversational dead-end with me. The conversation keeps rolling if you keep on trying to understand me and my viewpoint with no judgment. As soon as judgement or disagreement sets in, I end up arguing my corner and you argue yours. But how do you keep the conversation rolling?

Reflection

The most important tool you have in maintaining your neutrality is the tool of reflection- reflecting back at me what I have said. It provides you with something to say when you don't know what to say, and particularly when you disagree with what I have said.

Rather than entering a debate with me where I end up giving arguments against change and being more resistant, you avoid challenging me and 'roll with the resistance'. By reflecting you end up using my momentum to further explore my views and most importantly you keep the conversation going.

For example, if I say, *"I wouldn't have smashed up my room if my stupid foster carer hadn't been such a cow."* you can respond with, *"You're upset with your foster carer"* [reflects the emotion] or *"The reason you smashed up your room is because of your foster carer"* [restates their statement].

You aren't agreeing or disagreeing with me and stalling the conversation. Instead, you are inviting me to say more.

It is an important tool of understanding as well as a means for keeping the conversation going as it is often only when I hear what I have said reflected back to me that I can see for myself that my thinking is confused, incomplete or contradictory.

Open-ended questions

The use of carefully worded open-ended questions after I've said more can also help me to think through my own thinking and move the conversation forward.

Open-ended questions get way more out of me than closed questions and cause me to really reflect on my life, my thoughts and my actions. They can also provide you with valuable information on what might motivate me to change.

For example, it is easy to see that the closed question, *"Do you think taking drugs is a problem?"* will result in far less reflection and information than the open question, *"What has taking drugs done for you, positive and negative?"*

In addition, closed questions can end up with me feeling like you are trying to trick me into accepting your way of thinking or a particular intervention or treatment. Open questions are far better for increasing my internal motivation to change as they help me to reflect on my behaviour.

Open-ended questions can also provide opportunities for you to present me with some additional generalised information that I can take or leave in my reflections. You can then ask what I make of it, which provides me with an opportunity to consider, in an unthreatening way, how it relates to me.

For example, *"Some users of Pingers (Ecstasy) have reported that it makes them irritable and more likely to get angry. What's your experience?"*

Reframing statements

In addition to reflections and open-ended questions, reframing of statements can also shift conversations from resistance to considering change. They essentially show me that you are listening while also introducing the idea of change. This can be seen in the following examples:

'My Dad pisses me off so bad. He is always on my case, always.'

'Your Dad is really annoying you. (Emotive Reflection) I wonder if there is some way to get him to give you more positive attention rather than just negative?' (Reframe)

'Well what did he expect? Get in my face like that and he

has to expect me to hit him.'

'So you feel he was winding you up (Emotive Reflection). What else might he have expected? Is there any other way you could have dealt with that?' (Reframe)

PERSUASION OUT, PATIENCE IN

So if I'm resistant to the idea of change, don't try to argue with me or persuade me or judge me, it only encourages me to focus on why I don't want to change and to engage in resistance talk. Your focus instead should be on neutrally exploring my viewpoint and guiding me to think about reasons for change, what that change might look like and how it might be achieved.

If you dive in and try and fix me before I've even decided that there is something wrong that needs to be fixed then you might as well be talking to yourself. You have to start with me where I am and most teens like me will be pre-contemplative or contemplative at best.

You need to start with me where I am, not where you want me to be.

Don't get me wrong. This approach is no easy or quick fix. If I am one of your more disengaged teens, one of the most resistant to change, you will need a truckload of patience. There will be no overnight cure.

The key to it all is to stop being impatient, no matter how urgent the resolution of the issue might seem to you. You need to take the time to listen to me, to explore ideas with me and to try and understand me more, to understand how I tick without judging me. You need to start with me where I am, not where you want me to be.

Telling me what I should do because that seems like the quickest way to effect change and get me to your desired destination is going to have the exact opposite effect. The only person who can make the change is me and engaging in debate or argument pushes me further away, not nearer to change. All you can do is guide me, provide me with helpful information and help me to understand myself better so that I can make better decisions for myself. If you do this for me, I am way more likely to see the point of making a change and I am way more likely to see it through. The final destination might not be what you expect, but because it is my destination, decided by me, it will fit me better than anything you try to impose on me and makes it more likely that the changes will stick as my motivation for change has come from within.

The whole process begins and ends with me. Remember this and you'll help more teens like me than ever before, I promise.

The strategies described in this chapter are part of the Motivational Interviewing approach which emphasises the eliciting and strengthening of internal motivation for change. For more information on this method and appropriate techniques to use for each of the stages of change, visit:

http://www.teenagewhisperer.co.uk/WINFY.

References:

Bauer, J.S. et al (2008) 'Adolescent change language within a brief motivational intervention and substance use outcome', Psychology of Addictive Behaviors, 22:570-575

Brehm, J.W. (1966) A theory of psychological reactance (London: Academic Press)

Prochaska, J.O. & DiClemente, C.C. (1983) 'Stages and processes of self-change of smoking: Toward an integrative model of change', Journal of Consulting and Clinical Psychology 51(3):390-395

CREATIVE THINKING, CREATIVE SOLUTIONS, CREATIVE CHANGE

When was the last time you did something creative- made something, engaged in creative writing, acted, sang or danced? And when was the last time you did any of the above in a session with a young person?

Why? What does it matter, you may ask? Well your ability to help them change their lives has a lot to do with it actually.

Take this everyday example... If you want to change something, like the colour of your living room, you need to have an idea of what you want to change it to in order for it to actually happen. It's not until you've decided what colour you want it to be that you will actually go to the DIY store, purchase the paint and put it on the walls, right? You don't randomly and blindly buy the paint, take it home, put it on the walls and then decide that's the colour you want do you? No, you make that choice before you institute the change. And what do you need to make that choice? Some creativity! In order to have even a vague idea of what colour you want your living room to be, you need to engage in a bit of visualisation- imagining what it would look like in certain colours. So you have to get your creative juices flowing.

Now for some, creativity comes more easily than for others, but we do all have it in us and it can be fostered and encouraged. Which brings me back to the question of whether you are actively creative and whether you engage in creative activities in your sessions?

In working with difficult young people you are encouraging them to change- to try on a different behavioural colour or style. One of the problems is that they lack the tools to even begin to contemplate, let alone action change. Contemplation requires creative thinking, the ability to see beyond what is right underneath their noses, in their immediate frame of reference. And this is where the importance of creative activities comes in. These activities do not have to specifically be addressing an issue in their lives. The creative act in its own right is a therapeutic tool.

Creativity enables them to escape from the confines of the here and now and to dream and visualise something new. That could be something indirect like a piece of artwork showing what they think heaven and hell look like (which could also reveal some issues they have), or something more direct, like drawing a picture of what they want to be doing in five years' time.

Through creative activities you can help them to become dream-makers by helping them to get the creative parts of their brains going. In so doing you help them develop the ability to form dreams for their own lives so that they can work towards making them true.

So many kids have had dreams beaten out of them by discouraging at best, abusive at worst, parents, workers, teachers etc. We need to help them get that part of their brains up and running. Dreams form an escape from the harsh realities of life now, and provides them with a vision for their futures. (A fantastic example of this can be seen in the film 'Precious'. Here dreaming as an escape and the role of journaling for envisioning a better future are explored).

Creative activities not only help them to form dreams, but it also gives them a safe environment to explore new ideas and concepts and ways of doing things. Going back to our living room wall- it's always good to get some tester pots!

For example, by going to a street dance workshop they can learn new ways of using their bodies. While that might not sound like the biggest deal, doing anything new for a disengaged young person is a *massive* deal, and opens them up to the possibility of something new, of change. More directly, writing a poem or a song exploring how they could and should deal with a confrontational situation rather than their usual violent one and the feelings involved helps them to think through the practicalities and realities of change. This makes it more likely that they will give it a go as they will feel better equipped to deal with the pressures associated with change. Another obvious approach would be drama: using roleplay as a means of exploration.

Being creative also obviously involves the creation of something and when a young person creates something the immediate environment around them changes. A park looks different with a wall mural, the feeling in a room changes with the energy of a dance routine, a roomful of people can feel happier or more sad depending on a piece of music or a song. Through assisting them in the creation of something you are showing young people how they can affect the environment around them. While this is a valuable lesson in terms of the effects of their negative behaviour, it is extraordinarily powerful in terms of the positive effects they can have. You can show them that they are not inert powerless individuals, they can create and recreate things, and that includes themselves. They have the ability to recreate themselves for the better.

Obviously before you start a creative activity with a young person you have to consider what activity would be most appropriate according to their interests and ability to engage in group work or not. You also have to be mindful of the fact that creativity is a risk business for them. They may fear failure, or just 'looking like a dick'. Everyone has a level of fear when it comes to trying something new (and you are lying if you say you have absolutely none) so pitching the level of exposure in the activity to the person is key. So for someone who is painfully fearful, a smaller scale one-to-one creative activity would be better than a large group one.

Show me I can create and re-create things, and that includes myself.

And don't just sit there and watch them doing the creating. Aside from the fact that that is extremely nerve-wracking for them, it is not setting a good example. It implies (rightly or wrongly) that you are scared to get involved and try new things out which goes completely against what you are trying to achieve with them in their lives. You are an extremely important role model.

So help them be creative- it will reap dividends in helping them to help themselves. Yes, creative sessions do often require more thought, preparation and planning than your usual ones, but I promise you that by you using your creativity to come up with those sessions that you will be revitalised and re-energised for your work. I really truly believe that creativity feeds the soul. So it's a win-win.

ARE WE A JOKE? LIKED BUT A LIABILITY?

They love you. They think you're a great laugh. You're the cool one, the laid back one. The one who can shoot the breeze with the best of them. As great as the relationship may seem though, we always have to ask the question of ourselves- is this where it begins and ends? Are we doing everything we can to help our teens, to help them get to the point of change, of progressing and growing as individuals?

Don't get me wrong, good relationship building is at the core of what we do. Shooting the breeze, having a laugh, playing pool, kicking a ball about is where that starts, is where we appear human, is where the possibility of meaningful connection, of meaningful work, of meaningful exploration begins. None of the real work can start unless they think we're alright, that we are interested in them, that we actually might care. No arguments, this part is vitally important.

The problem comes when this working relationship 'story' never progresses beyond the first paragraph. When we don't get into depth of character, into fully exploring their story and how we can help them progress in their lives. When we don't get anywhere near resolving the issues, the plots, the twists of their story before the final page with them is turned.

We are then their buddy, nothing more, nothing less. They see us as pure equals, just like them. Our ability to help them change is seriously diminished as they do not see us as a source of caring expertise, as people with ideas and some life experiences that might help them out. We render ourselves fairly impotent.

I don't need a pal with no point, I need an agent of change.

Striking the right balance is not easy. For some teens, just the process of building a relationship of trust is a massive step in and of itself and so more time does need to be spent on helping them get comfortable in our company. But if we are to stand any real hope of helping them we need to always have our eyes on the goal, on what change we want to achieve. The getting comfortable part is the means to an end, not the end itself.

Sometimes we may not achieve the goal in the time-frame we have available to us as we can't rush it, but if we get to the end of our time with them and we never had at least our eyes on what we ultimately wanted to achieve with them (other than connection) then I would argue that we never stood a chance of getting there in the first place.

Sometimes we can underestimate their readiness to take the next step in the relationship, to start to tackle their issues. We can be afraid of taking the next step in case they turn away from us as they have so often done with others who have tried to help them.

In trying to strike the balance and in deciding when to take the next step we need to remind ourselves of the building blocks of relationship: what makes relationships, where real depth of connection and respect comes from and what holds those relationships together, even when the subject matter may be challenging and we have to face their behaviour head-on. Once we have grasped this we avoid being merely the pal with no point as we have the confidence to take the relationship further, tackle the issues and become the caring agent of change that our teens so desperately need.

RELATIONSHIP BUILDING BLOCKS

The magnetism of care

If we really do care about our teens, it will show. If we have taken the time to get to know them as people rather than as a problem then they should feel human in our company. For many the sense, even if not rationally understood, that someone cares will keep them coming back for more, particularly when care has been in short supply in their lives. So when we do move on to explore their lives and their issues more closely it will seem less like an interrogation, a violation, and more like an information gathering exercise by someone who wants to understand and use that information to help them, rather than trip them up.

Listening promotes talking

They may well resist at first as they will still be operating on old information- that we are just one of those meddling workers like they've had before who are hell bent on fixing their problem without seeing them. In these situations, emphasising our listening role in the relationship can help to break down any barriers. Things like open-ended questions, letting the conversation at first go in the direction they want to take it. It's easier to redirect something that is moving than something that is all gummed up, standing stock still. No judgements, no opinions from us at first, just rolling with it. (See the chapter, 'Non-Judgementalism: Start With Me Where I Am', for more on Motivational Interviewing techniques).

Respect allows caring challenge

Once they feel listened to, our teens will feel respected and they will come to respect us in return. Then the possibility of respectful caring challenge comes into play. Rather than just listening, more challenging enquiries can be made. Questions along the line of, 'Do you think that is appropriate?', 'How do you think that made them feel?'. We are not passing our own judgement but asking them to reflect for themselves.

If we ask them these questions straight off the bat, before the listening respect has been established they will chalk us up as judgmental clueless idiots who are just asking such questions to highlight how awful they are. Once respect has been established they will interpret those questions very differently, as genuine enquiries as to what they think, with no self-righteous judgmental overtones.

Teens aren't stupid and will know that we are likely to have certain opinions but if we have set the tone that this is about them, their experiences, thoughts and feelings then they are less likely to go on the defensive and are more likely to share, more likely to really consider what we are asking them to reflect upon. Perception is everything.

Boundaries as tools of care

Sometimes however certain circumstances will necessitate us taking a more explicitly authoritative role. Like when a young person needs to be breached from their supervision/probation order and sent back to court for failing to show up for statutory appointments or for throwing a wobbly at us, or being temporarily banned from a group activity for behaving inappropriately.

All of the above are always a possibility even when we have been making major progress. And this is where many a worker becomes unstuck. They have made great strides in connecting with a young person and then inappropriate, unacceptable behaviour rears its head. And the worker decides that in light of progress made that they will effectively ignore it. They won't breach them from their court order, they won't temporarily ban them from the group, they won't follow standard protocol. They'll have a word with them and then effectively turn a blind eye; we wouldn't want to wreck the relationship, the progress made would we?

But in doing this a valuable opportunity is wasted. If a good relationship has been built, progress made, then a learning opportunity about boundaries as boundaries of care has been lost.

For many teens, they have never had the security that comes from consistency, from knowing limits. When people who care create and enforce boundaries, then the child knows where it stands. They know if they do x, y will happen. If there is no consistency, they are left wondering what the response will be which is particularly unsettling if a parent or carer tends to have erratic mood swings. Or they will know that they can do what the hell they want because their parent or carer doesn't actually care about what they do because they don't really care about them. Either way, mental insecurity ensues.

Some teens will have had boundaries used against them as weapons of hate rather than as tools of care. They'll have had a teacher who hates the ground they walk on, enforce some rule that isn't their standard protocol and punish them just to inflict pain. Or they'll have experienced a prison officer use unjustified violence against them for the slightest infraction, like talking in line when they are supposed to be silent.

So some teens have never known what it is to be cared about enough to have a boundary enforced. Others have learned that boundaries and rules are tools of oppression.

Boundaries exist in life, they are what orders society and stops it from descending into chaos; they keep people safe and feeling secure. So by not showing teens why boundaries exist, that this is the way society orders itself, and demonstrating how they are supposed to be used, we deny them the opportunity to learn how to get along in society and to progress as individuals. And we deny them the opportunity to know that we want to keep them safe, we want them to feel secure and that is because we care about them.

So if a boundary is enforced in a caring way, where time is taken to explain why we are doing it then the relationship does not have to suffer because we are still meeting their ultimate need for care.

In my personal experience, when I have had to breach teens from their court supervision/probation orders for various reasons including not showing up, mouthing off, threatening behaviour, I have seen growth and progress in the relationship, not deterioration. Once the immediate dust has settled I always take the time to explain how pleased I  am with any progress that has been made, how I am enjoying getting to know them and why I am breaching them and sending them back to court (unacceptable behaviour = standard response = follow protocol).

Nine times out of ten I get an apology, which I then include in my report for court, which obviously helps them no end and usually they are allowed to continue on their order. One time out of ten I'll get an earful, a full on teen tantrum. But somewhere down the line, even if it's after a stint in custody, they calm down and we'll pick back up where we left off.

As long as I always behave with integrity, consistency and respect towards them, I always earn it back. They know I care about them and they know that I am fair and that is the knowledge that ultimately wins the day in their heads. They come to realise that if I had not breached them when others are breached for the same behaviour that I would actually be unfair, which would place doubt in their minds as to whether they could trust me, because they wouldn't know which way I might swing in my response to their behaviour. My consistency of response keeps them feeling safe in the relationship, even when the potential physical consequences of incarceration may make them feel unsafe. They always know where they stand with me and that always keeps the relationship going.

And this consistency of care reaps dividends. It can cause kids to turn up to court to face their breach when usually they'd go on the run. It can cause them to pluck up the courage to speak to the magistrates and apologise, to ask them to let them continue on their orders because they feel they are making progress. Or it can cause the teen who serves some time for their misdemeanour to still turn up for their first appointment 'on the out'.

THE LIABILITY OF PLACING TOO MUCH EMPHASIS ON BEING LIKED

The alternative to this can be heard in youth court waiting rooms up and down the country where conversation often turns to discussing statutory workers- Youth Offending Team workers, social workers etc. I've anonymously sat in the middle of it on many an occasion and even when you control for teen bravado, the results are clear:

Young person chatting to friend: *'He's total safe. It's great. We do f*** all. He knows not to mess man. He knows not to mess. He even lets me win pool most times. Total pussy'.*

Young person speaking to another young person who is in court on breach: *'Oh my days, she's whippin' you. You're her bitch man! Missed two appointments? That's how many I turn up to! I jus' roll with my shit and rock up to YOT*

(Youth Offending Team) when I'm in the code (postcode). I'm a busy man. They run with my office hours. I'm tellin' you, you need to get my worker man.'

Who do we want to be? The one who cares enough to make the tough decisions, or the one who doesn't? The one that gets teens closer to change, or the one who doesn't? The one who appears on the surface of it to be widely liked or the one that is deeply liked? The one that is seen as tough but fair and ultimately caring, or the one who is, quite frankly, a joke?

If we are just their buddy or mate, then we limit our potential as workers and we also limit their potential to learn, to grow, to change, to feel really cared for, to be in a stable, predictable relationship. And when it comes to the tough decisions, the boundary enforcements, we can be at risk of becoming the joke if we don't make the right choice. When we don't enforce the boundary it is then that we become complicit because we end up helping them continue in their negative behaviour and avoiding addressing their issues. We are not helping, we are hindering.

So we need to consider each and every day, could anyone say of us, *'I can do what the f*** I like with this one.'* If so, maybe we need to consider if we are too much of a friend and not enough of a helper. Friends are widely available, real helpers are in short supply. I know which one I'd rather be, and I know which one deep down they'd rather we were too.

STRENGTH IN NUMBERS

You keep on telling me that I can't do this on my own, that I need a support network. That I need to have people I can ask for help, people I can talk to, people just around to help me out. People to talk to about my problems, to help me come up with solutions. You might have taken me to play a team sport or build a raft, all in the name of helping me to see that when I work with others to solve problems or achieve a goal, better solutions result. You've even told me that *"Two heads are better than one"*, or *"No man, woman, boy or girl is an island."* Okay, okay, I get it. But in all of this, do you?

I ask you this, because your ability to help me depends massively on your ability to collaborate and work with others. It also depends on your willingness to allow yourself to be supported by others.

I am a complex ball of emotions, of behaviours, of pain, of

confusion- that's why you are working with me. To expect that you as one person can gather all the relevant information about me to be able to work out how best to help me is asking too much of yourself. You need to be a top class information gatherer, and the best information gatherers are those that involve as many people as possible. So you need to be talking to school, to tutors, heads of year or house, to social workers, to any therapists who have previously been involved, to family, to police, to youth offending services, to anyone I am involved with. This way, combined with you asking me about my take on my life and behaviour and issues, you get the broadest possible picture of me.

Maybe I behave brilliantly in certain situations or with certain people, but am terrible with others. Which can then lead you to ask why this is the case and to unpick what my particular issues are. Some people will leave out important pieces of information, intentionally or unintentionally, that others will fill in for you. Your approach when helping me will only be as good as the information you have at your disposal.

And the process of information gathering will cause you to make connections with people which will usually lead to closer collaborative working. You are all working towards the common goal of helping me and that is easier and more effective when you are continually information sharing and coming up with joint, consistent strategies. Joined up thinking I think you call it.

To expect that you, one person, will have all the answers is impossible. In fact it's ridiculous. You all come to the table with different training, specialities and expertise so your approaches and ideas will be different- which is exactly what I need. Your best chance of reaching me is often when an assortment of approaches are used. Some will work, some won't, but it is in combining resources and approaches that you find out what does work. If you just come to me with only your ideas or your approach you are already limiting the likelihood of success.

So for some, lots of talking therapy might help, for others it's practical activities like climbing or regular gym trips or gardening that help more, for some it's a combination. For some mindfulness might be the golden bullet, for others it's the unveiling of a longstanding

If you just come to me with only your ideas or your approach you are already limiting the likelihood of success.

learning difficulty such as dyslexia or a diagnosis of ADHD or autism and getting the help they really need. And to find all this out, I will usually need a team of people to help. One worker might have expertise in one area, another a different area. You'll all be able to share strategies and knowledge with the rest. You will all become more knowledgeable about me, and also become more knowledgeable about strategies to help other young people like me. You grow in your work as you help me to grow. It's collaborative growth.

And you know what happens when you pull together and join resources? You all seem more enthusiastic, energised and focused and hopeful, which also increases the chances of reaching me, because enthusiasm, energy and hope are so contagious! So you feel better about your work and I begin to feel cared for and supported because I have a team of people around me. It's collaborative enthusiasm and care.

But so many of you workers don't do this. I see you each as

individual people, as my teacher, my counsellor, my social worker, my youth worker but you don't really communicate. You go along in your bubbles, repeat the same work with me and cause me to fall off the 'boredom cliff' where I just stop listening to you. Or I have the same game-plan with each of you to try and avoid addressing my issues, that doesn't mean much to you in isolation. If you would only communicate you would realise I say and do the same things with all of you, there is a pattern, a need to be addressed. Problem is that once in a blue moon two of you might end up in a meeting together, but this is rarer than it should be and you don't really talk and don't really share information and ideas. Your ability to help me is compromised.

So I've got another question for you? Why don't you collaborate more? What's standing in the way of you doing this?

And if you think about this, the answer for you is exactly the same as me. The reason why I don't like asking for help, why I don't go much for teamwork, for building a support network is because I'm scared. If I reach out and share with someone I am putting myself on the line. I am making myself vulnerable and accepting that I can't do it on my own, and that is scary, so very scary.

Some guy, Patrick Lencioni once said, "Teamwork begins by building trust. And the only way to do that is to overcome our need for invulnerability."

You in your professional boots might want other professionals to look at you and think how good you are and how knowledgeable you are. You might think that to ask others for information and ideas is to make you seem less important, less knowledgeable. Or if you're a bit stuck with your work with me, and want some advice, you might think that to ask another is to expose yourself as incompetent or a fraud. But can I let you in on something I've learned? People aren't generally out there looking to see someone's flaws; they are looking to make a connection. So the worker that says, 'hey, can I pick your brain on Joe?' is not seen as incompetent, they are seen as open and friendly, someone passionately committed to helping young people like me.

By reaching out we grow in other people's eyes, we don't diminish.

And it's not just other workers that see this, I see it too. If you bring other people in to help me, or get everybody singing from the same song sheet with me, I will know at least on a subconscious level that you all really care. Rather than one person trying to do a solo that is mediocre, I see a choir of people trying to help, all singing the same song. Even if all have a mediocre voice, the resulting sound is better than each part and I'll be more likely to listen.

And you know what else? By collaborating with others, a worker is seen as an expert at helping young people precisely because they know how important collaborative working is. And I know this because I've found that when I reach out to other people, to ask for their support and advice, I am viewed as mature, as having developed great social skills and coping skills, rather than a naïve struggling teen. By reaching out we grow in other people's eyes, we don't diminish.

So we have to take that step to share ideas and ask for

advice. We have to trust in the best of people and not the worst. It's like that guy Patrick said, teamwork begins with trust. We have to trust that if we make ourselves a bit vulnerable and accept we don't know everything, that good will come of it, not bad. And I've found this to be true, and I reckon me asking for help made me way more vulnerable than if you do it. If I can do it, then so can you. You'll help so many more teens this way.

Or maybe this isn't your problem with teamwork? Maybe you think that you really *do* know it all? To this I can only say that nobody knows everything. If you expect me to accept help and advice, to accept I don't have all the answers, then you have to do the same, or you're just a hypocrite. Trust me, I can spot hypocrisy and insincerity a mile off and it will damage our relationship.

When I wasn't accepting help from others and was taking a misguided arrogant 'I know what I'm doing, I don't want any help' view, I was asked to consider whether I was afraid of lowering my barriers and letting someone else in. Do you think this could be your problem too? Is your arrogance a mask for fear?

If so, like I said before, you need to make yourself comfortable with the idea of being vulnerable, because that is how we successfully connect with others in all aspects of life. It happens when our guard is down and we talk openly and honestly. You'll form better connections with people than ever before, including the teens you work with because you'll go from being an untouchable (pretend) superhuman, to a normal human people can connect with. And because you'll end up sharing and collaborating you'll get smarter and more knowledgeable and you'll grow instead of being arrogant and stagnating. It's a no-brainer.

Or maybe you don't involve others in your work with troubled teens because you just don't have the time. I'm sorry but just as you call 'bulls*** alert' on stuff I say, I'm calling it right back at you. If you are serious about helping me then you don't have the time *not* to collaborate. The best, most efficient workers are the ones that are the most resourceful and other professionals are a most precious resource. In one phone call or meeting you will find out more about me than you could spending the equivalent time reading a file on me. In talking, you get the headlines about me, get to know the most important pressing matters, get to find out ways of connecting with me that no file can tell you in the same way. This is efficient working.

Plus, if you have a network of professionals trying to help, you have a team of people to call upon when things crop up. Like when my Mum has to unexpectedly go into hospital and I'm dumped at a relative's and I need some reassurance, some support, just to know people care. Rather than reaching out just being 'on' one of you, it's a task that any one of you can do, dependent on workloads, location, leave etc. And with good give-and-take the load is shared. Collaboration is a no-brainer for you as well as me. For everyone, a problem shared is a problem halved.

And it's not just help with the practical stuff that you benefit from when you collaborate with others. You might actually make some friends that you can call upon when you need a bit of emotional support, a friendly ear, some re-motivation or perspective on an issue from someone who has an idea of what you might be going through. So collaboration is also an important part of self-care, which let's face it, when you're working with challenging young people like me is something you can't afford to forget. You need others to help you, just like I need others to help me.

Connecting with others is vital for all of us. It helps us personally, provides us with support networks, with advice and ideas. It expands our worlds rather than leaving us stuck in our own heads and for you, stuck in your own caseload. It creates opportunities that we would never have access to if we stay locked up in our own little worlds. And for you, collaboration can enable you to help me, to reach me and to make a real difference. Your collaborating and reaching out can literally change my world. Do you care enough to do it?

HOPE-FILLED VISION

WHEN WORKING WITH SOME TEENS SEEMS POINTLESS

Working relationships with young people can be so transient, and particularly so with troubled teens. There's the relentless change in their circumstances and their behaviour. The change in the ability and willingness of our organisations and the individuals in them to continue working with them.

All these factors mean that we can often struggle to believe that we are making any difference in their lives. Our time with them is a tiny drop in a vast, vast ocean. It can feel like we can't make any difference, have any meaningful impact in such a short amount of time. It can feel like we are fulfilling a time requirement, or just waiting for them to stuff up and be moved on.

And no matter how hard we try, no matter how hard we try to make a difference it can sometimes seem like we are talking to ourselves and that we are not getting through. The lines of superficial communication may be open, there may be words being exchanged, but their behaviour doesn't seem to be improving.

From here a sense of futility and pointlessness can so easily set in, particularly when we know that we aren't going to be working with them for long enough to turn things around. Alternatively we might have been working with them for so long and nothing has changed, and a cynicism has set in, 'nothing has changed up till now, it's just not going to happen. They are a lost cause'.

These are the young people that are the tough nuts to crack. We just can't seem to get past the hard shells to connect with their true inner beings rather than the façade; to see them, to know them and to help them with their hurts, their pains, to share in their hopes, their dreams. We don't seem to be really communicating, aside from some grunts, some 'dunno's, some swear words, or some lip-service responses that they think have tricked you into thinking that they are really contemplating change.

So what to do? How do we stop ourselves from not really trying any more, giving up, declaring defeat in our minds and just going through the motions of an intervention? Why should we keep on trying, is there any point? Are there just some who will always be beyond our reach?

To all of this, there is one response: We have to see beyond the here and now. Beyond the behaviour that is in front of us, beyond the barriers that they have thrown up around themselves, beyond this moment in their lives. We have to look beyond our relationship or lack of it now.

We have to become less hung up on seeing results for ourselves right now, because it is there that disappointment and disenchantment often lies. We have to take a long term view of our work with them, even if our work with them is very short.

With the most challenging young people, it is key that we see our work as sowing seeds, not necessarily reaping a harvest. Sowing seeds of ideas about themselves, like their potential for change, their ability to take control of their lives, their ability to get over their trauma, that they can be who they want to be, they are worthy, they are loveable. The seeds of ideas about life, like that change is a challenge for everyone, or the seeds of ideas about doing things differently, like responding to people and situations differently rather than just reacting.

We may have time to sow one seed or ten, but as long as we are constantly at least trying to sow seeds then we will always have purpose, there is never futility in our actions, there is never a young person beyond hope. Because seeds are agents of transformation.

Seeds are seemingly nothing and can be mistaken for specks of dirt, but they have such potential within them. At the right time, in the right place, with the right circumstances they can change from nothing into something. They can transform into a thriving, living plant.

The here and now with a young person may well not be the right time, the right place, the right circumstances for them to hear what you are saying and to take it on board. The seeds you are sowing may be currently falling on unfertile ground. But seeds can lie dormant for years before germinating. The structure of the soil may change, the light and rain conditions may change, what was once an arid desert might become a fertile plant-loving oasis. And those seeds have the potential to germinate.

You probably won't be around to see it. A large amount of the time you won't see it or get to hear of it. It may take ten, twenty, thirty years. It may even happen beyond our lifetimes, with a realisation occurring when that young person is in their last phase of life. You may witness them get a lot worse like when you see their face in adulthood on your local police's 'Most Wanted' list and you may increasingly doubt that it will ever happen. A lot of the time it probably doesn't happen. But the key thing is- we do not know. We do not know what lies ahead.

The not knowing enables us to have hope. Hope that the germination will come, the hope that our young people will reap a harvest at some point in their lives. And this is the gift that should keep us going, should keep us helping, should keep us motivated when we are not getting the best immediate feedback from our young people.

We can sow seeds with purpose because we hope. We hope for a better time, a better place, a more receptive fertile ground. We can do what we do despite the swearing, despite the setbacks, despite the disappointments, quite simply if we believe in the power of seeds.

My life was changed by a seed that was sown when I was in my teens. Some words were said to me at the age of 15 that although they kind of washed over me at the time and didn't have any real significance, turned out to be the most significant words of my life.

Someone told me that I was beautiful on the inside. At the time I didn't realise that I actually had low self-esteem, so these words meant little to me. I don't think I comprehended that I should think I was beautiful on the inside. Surely that would be a bit big-headed? So the words flew over the top of my head and left me, or so I thought.

However at a time in my twenties when I had come to realise that I did in fact have hideously low self-esteem and doubted my worth, those words returned to me. To this day they sustain me when I doubt myself. And somebody sowed that seed. It fell on unfertile ground and lay dormant for years. But in the right circumstances, when my thinking was in the right place, it germinated.

And our words and actions towards the young people that we work with can sow seeds in exactly the same way. We just have to believe, to have patience, to have hope.

I was fortunate enough to have a young person make contact with me some years after I had worked with her. Wow, at the time she was *hard* work. Like fingers screeching down the blackboard hard work. I'd despair. I seemed to have to be constantly warning her that her behaviour was going to put her in breach of her bail conditions or her community sentences, or would be filling out the paperwork when I had to follow through. Half the time she'd turn up to our sessions off her head on some chemical concoction, or else be in an unworkable state on the come-down. In a few sessions she was on more of an even keel and we did manage to actually talk.

In one of those sessions I told her that she did not have to let her life be defined by her past experience of sexual abuse, that she was more than what had happened to her. She could hide from her pain with drink and drugs, but that she would still be living her life based on what had happened to her and not living it on her terms. She told me to *'f*** off'*, and *'what do you know?'*. She ended up moving away and that was the last I heard from her, until about five years later.

Much to my surprise, she got in contact to say *'thank you'*, to say that even though she was a nightmare that I always tried to help. And she told me that the words, *'don't let yourself be defined by your past'* had stuck with her, and they just wouldn't go away. Eventually she realised that something had to change so that she could actually live her life for her, and so she had taken the steps to stop drinking and using, to seek help in processing her experiences of abuse. As a result she was now clean, not offending and had got herself a steady job in a shop that she really enjoyed. She had turned her life around. The seed had germinated, she sought the help that she needed from others and allowed them to sow further seeds, and the harvest had come.

I was so fortunate to have found out about this, that she went to the effort to make contact. This is extremely unusual and we can't work expecting to see these results, to get this feedback. If we are in this for personal glory, for trophy teens that we can point at and say 'Look how I helped them', then we will be sadly disappointed.

Particularly with the toughest teens, we will most likely not be around to see the fruits of our labours. Sometimes we will, which is great, but mostly we won't. It may take further seeds being sown by other people further down the line, for the harvest to fully come.

We have to take it on trust that there is always the possibility of germination, of growth, of harvest. If we have that, then we will work harder and work smarter, even with our most challenging teens, even when we don't have long with them or when they seem like a lost cause, because there is always hope that a seed we sow will germinate at some point in the future.

We have to look beyond the here and now and remember that through the sowing of seeds we are working with

young people's futures as much as we are working with
them now.

LIKE WHAT YOU'VE READ?

Read more from Sam Ross in

ANGER IS MY FRIEND: Rethinking Teen Anger Management

READ THE FIRST CHAPTER FOR FREE ON THE NEXT PAGE!

AVAILABLE NOW AT AMAZON

TO FIND OUT MORE VISIT:
WWW.TEENAGEWHISPERER.CO.UK/ANGER

EXCERPT FROM
'ANGER IS MY FRIEND:
RETHINKING TEEN ANGER MANAGEMENT'

You probably don't realise this, but anger is my friend. My best friend. It's my certainty amidst uncertainty. It's always there for me, it protects me. It tells me I'm alive. It shows me that I exist in other people's worlds. And you know what? It often makes me feel good, real good. It shows I have some power, some real raw power within me and I don't get that any other time. For those few moments I can be king of the world and no-one can take that from me.

It's my emotional rock in a sea of mixed up feelings that I have no way of understanding or processing. I love my Mum but she's crap. I love my Dad but he's a loser who doesn't care about me, I don't even know where he is. I really like some of my teachers and we can have a bit of a laugh. But I'm scared, really scared that maybe they'll get too close and see how vulnerable I am. Or my mates will think I'm pathetic for getting on with them so well. Or my Mum will be angry and think that I'm trying to replace her or something. Or maybe they'll end up finding me annoying and will reject me.

I don't know how to express all this, I'm not even aware of most of it. I need to express something, and as my head is whirring with all these thoughts I seem to have no control over and don't fit in my head, I end up blowing my top- I get angry. Me being angry with me for having such conflicting thoughts. Me being angry with you for making me feel this way with your kindness, your nagging, basically whatever you do.

So amidst this blur of conflicting emotions I have a rock, a default feeling I can fall back on, one I can easily express even when all the others are confused. Even though it looks like my storm, it's not, it's my safe port. My anger, my best friend.

It protects me. It wraps me in ten layers of bubble-wrap and no amount of popping is going to let you get to me. Deep down I do want you to see my pain and my conflicting emotions and help me process them but I'm scared, so if I sense you're getting too close I will push you away. I will find a reason to erupt, a reason for me to hate you and a reason for you to run.

I don't want to expose myself to the risk of being hurt or rejected again. I'm terrified that you'll see the real me, will think I'm crazy, will be shocked, completely horrified. So I'll erect my big fat anger diversion sign and send you off down the road where you can dump me. It leaves me to sit in my bubble-wrap, protected from the world once more. My anger, my friend.

The thing is I know exactly what to expect from you if I blow up. It's beautifully predictable. I push you away, you push me away. It's my certainty amidst my emotional chaos. I control the end result. I might not be in control of my head but this I am in control of. My anger, my steady friend.

Anger also makes me feel alive. When I get that sick

feeling in my stomach, or my face feels hot and flushed and my heart is beating like a high-speed train I know that I live. I feel like such a nobody that sometimes I wonder if I exist. But when those anger juices start pumping I am in no doubt. I don't feel like a shell of a person any more, I don't feel empty. So my anger fills me, it fills my void. Where security, stability, love, happiness, self-worth and purpose should live, there lives my anger. I'll take anger over emptiness any day. My anger knows I live.

And when I get a reaction from you I know I exist, not just in my own skin, but I exist in your world too. I make it onto your radar. And wow, that gives me a buzz. I might feel stupid and embarrassed after, further adding to my confused feelings, but at the time it feels great. Hell, I actually have some power for once. I really do exist.

To see you getting angry right back at me, to see you squirm when I hurl an insult, to see you struggle to regain control, to see you have to call for backup; it shows I have some influence. It shows I can make people notice and think about me.

It shows I can make people do what I want them to, like chuck me out of the classroom when I really can't do the work and don't want everyone to see that; to make you push me away if I feel you are getting too close; to make you stop talking about that thing that really upsets me. And you know what one of the cleverest parts of me being angry is? I can make you feel what I feel. I can make you feel insecure, frustrated, vulnerable, useless, scared, out of control, confused. I can show you the friends of my anger. My anger, my best friend.

You should also know that feeling this power is addictive. Some people get addicted to drugs or alcohol to make them feel better, others to exercise, others to food, some to combinations of things. Well my primary addiction is my anger. It works for me on so many levels, or so it seems. My anger, my BFF.

Which is where you come in. You've probably been 'called in' to sort out my anger, to do some 'anger management' with me. Well shove right off.

Nothing makes me more angry than someone trying to fix my anger. It's like someone coming in and telling me that I need to kill my friend. When my back is against the wall and someone tries to take one of the last friends I have then I will tell you straight- get stuffed. You don't mess with me and you don't mess with my best mate.

If you really want to help me, you need to treat my anger for the friend it is. So just like you don't tell me not to do something cos you know it'll make me do it more, don't tell me to quit my anger cos it'll only push us closer together. What you've got to do is help me come to realise that the way my anger friend treats me isn't helping me in life, that I am actually held hostage by it and that there are better friends out there for me, other options. You then leave it to me to decide.

Cos the truth is that my anger actually chokes me when it has this addictive hold over me. Although I can be really noisy with it, it actually stops me from speaking and stops me from being really heard. It stops me from being able to properly connect with people and to even try to begin to explain myself and my feelings. It steals my emotional voice. It shoves a rag in my mouth and raps tape round my face.

So you've got to help me see this and this is no easy job. As you try to connect with me, my anger pushes back and tries to keep you out, stopping you from helping me. So expect a lot of angry outbursts from me at first. Get used to being told to 'fuck off'. Desensitise yourself to it. I don't really deep down mean it, this is my anger talking.

After a while me and my anger realise that you are not going away. That my anger doesn't always work at pushing you away. And then it will dawn on me that maybe my anger isn't that powerful after all. It might work well at getting me what I need at a particular moment, like you to get lost, or to make you feel like me, but it doesn't actually get me what I really want and need- a secure attachment to someone. A relationship with someone who I can really talk to, who I feel safe enough with to explore my emotional conflicts and confusion. And the thing is that as soon as I actually start talking about all this pent-up confusion, I gradually, bit by bit lose my reliance on my friend, my anger. Me and my friend begin to separate, our explosive relationship diminishes.

Once my anger with you loses its hold, I have a bit of room to breathe, room to explore my anger with everything and everyone else. I can then explore how I use anger to protect myself, to ensure predictability in how others treat me and then look for alternative ways of protecting myself.

I then might get to a place where I can begin to unwrap some of the excess layers of bubble-wrap around me so that I have the confidence to take the risk of 'putting myself out there' a bit more. I will then come to see that if I reveal more of myself to others, then we will better connect and my basic need for attachment will be met. I need to learn that emotional attachment doesn't have to be scary and negative, as it may have been in the past, and the benefits make it a risk worth taking.

Part of just talking with you will do that, it will be my first test-run at this. Next steps could be sharing with others like me who have made some progress in understanding their best friend, a sort of anger support group. We can then begin to share with others who 'get it'. I'll end up with some good mates this way who I really connect with which will further meet my base need for meaningful attachment. So rather than a bunch of 'angry mess-ups' in a room together being a recipe for disaster as adults so often think, it can really help us. We can find each other as friends and we can support each other. We can tell our destructive, disengaging anger 'friends' to take a hike.

You can help us prepare and cope with the unpredictability of life so we don't go nuts when things don't go our way, or how we expected them to. We won't then need to resort to the predictability of an anger exchange to try and regain control. Show us how spontaneity can be a good thing and that we don't need to be in complete control the whole time.

Validate our feelings of anger. We so often get told that our anger is wrong. Problem is that it is a huge part of us so telling us it is just plain wrong invalidates us. It's not our anger that is wrong, it is the way we inappropriately express it in the wrong situations. Help us to also see that often when we are angry it is not the situation in front of us that we are angry at, but something much deeper.

And this is where looking at our triggers in-depth helps. It helps us work this out. But you don't just help me discover what my triggers are, but also why they are my triggers. Once you help me do this then disentangling appropriate from inappropriate responses becomes much easier.

So 'anger management' doesn't have to involve completely kicking my good friend anger to the curb. He is a valid friend who does have a place in my life. I just have to make sure that he doesn't take over, doesn't control me, turns up for the right events in the right clothing and doesn't mess up my thinking and my actions.

My anger can be a particularly good friend in one area. When controlled by me and used appropriately, he can help me seek proper justice for events in my life. That is often why I am so angry- I'm angry at the injustice of things that have happened and happen to me. Problem is, in trying to voice my anger, I often direct it at the wrong person and in the wrong way. Show me how to do this the right way.

I can seek justice with my anger for events like being abused and reporting the perpetrator and ensuring it never happens again. Or seek justice for the little things, like getting angry that my worker never shows up on time and doesn't seem to care. Show me how to channel that anger into making an appropriate complaint. Help me to get justice by communicating in a way that gets the change I need. When I see positive results I am unlikely to turn to my destructive friend so regularly.

So help me turn my destructive, controlling, life-encompassing angry best friend into a positive, life-building, life-changing friend that only comes round when he's really needed. The process won't be easy, and I'll have my relapses, but I can get there.

Just remember that whenever talking to me or my mates about our anger, don't disrespect our friend and what we feel he does for us. Just help us see how he oversteps the mark and messes stuff up for us. Then we will put anger back in his place and change his role in our lives. We have a lot to be angry about, and its usually not the surface stuff you see. Help us harness the real root of our anger and help us use it for own and others' benefit. Make what seems like a bad friend, into something good.

SAM ROSS

BSc, MSc, MSc, Cert EP (YJ)

Sam Ross, popularly known as the 'Teenage Whisperer', is a Teen Behavioural Consultant, passionate about connecting with and helping the most challenging, disengaged and troubled teens to turn their lives around. She works in both educational and criminal justice settings, both with young people and their parents or carers. Really understanding teens is the beginning, middle and end of her work and she helps professionals and parents achieve this through her website, books and training.

To find out more about her work, to read her blog and to connect with her and other like-minded professionals please visit:

www.teenagewhisperer.co.uk

@Teen_Whisperer

www.facebook.com/teenagewhisperer

linkedin.com/in/teenagewhisperer/

Printed in Great Britain
by Amazon